**ISBN:** 979-8-9946438-0-8

# Security+ 2.0 | AI-Powered Mastery

CompTIA Security+ Exam Ready

*First Edition: January 2026*

Muhammad Iftikhar

# Disclaimer

This book is an independent publication and is not affiliated with, endorsed by, or sponsored by CompTIA®.

CompTIA®, Security+®, and related trademarks are the property of CompTIA, Inc.

This book is designed as a supplementary learning resource to support CompTIA Security+ exam preparation and real-world cybersecurity understanding.

# Dedication

In loving memory of my parents, *Muhammad Ishaq Uppal* and *Sughra Baigum,* everything I am today is because of you.

# Contents

# About the Author

Professor Muhammad Iftikhar, widely known as Professor Ifti, is an experienced Information Technology educator and cybersecurity professional with more than 25 years of combined industry and academic experience. He is currently pursuing a Ph.D. in Information Technology with an emphasis in Cyber Engineering, with academic and research interests focused on secure system design, identity and access management, cybersecurity architecture, and applied security education.

Professor Ifti serves as a full-time faculty member at Northern Virginia Community College (NOVA), where he teaches Information Technology, Cloud Computing, and Cybersecurity across academic and workforce development programs. His instructional approach emphasizes competency-based learning, certification alignment, scenario-driven instruction, and real-world applicability, preparing students for both industry certifications and operational cybersecurity roles.

He holds a Master of Science in Cybersecurity and Information Assurance, an MBA in Information Management, a Bachelor of Education, and a Bachelor of Science in Computer Science. Professor Iftikhar is also a graduate of the Harvard Bok Higher Education Teaching Certificate Program at Harvard University's Derek Bok Center for Teaching and Learning, where he developed expertise in learning science, inclusive pedagogy, and evidence-based instructional design.

Professor Iftikhar maintains an extensive portfolio of professional certifications, including CompTIA A+, Network+, Security+ CE, CySA+ CE, CSAP, Certified Ethical Hacker (CEH), Computer Hacking Forensic Investigator (CHFI), AWS Certified Cloud Practitioner, and multiple certifications in online and hybrid teaching. He regularly integrates exam objectives, performance-based questions (PBQs), applied labs, and AI-supported learning activities into his curriculum to bridge theory and practice.

In addition to teaching, Professor Iftikhar is actively engaged in curriculum development, instructional material authoring, and faculty collaboration, with a focus on scalable, high-quality cybersecurity education for diverse learner populations. He maintains a professional resource platform at www.ProfessorIfti.com, where he shares instructional materials, certification resources, and cybersecurity learning tools.

# Preface

Cybersecurity education is evolving. Traditional textbooks alone are no longer sufficient to prepare learners for modern threats, adaptive technologies, and real-world decision-making. While the CompTIA Security+ certification remains a critical milestone for aspiring cybersecurity professionals, success today requires more than memorization—it requires *critical thinking, visualization, and continuous learning.*

*Security+ 2.0 | AI-Powered Mastery for Next-Gen Cybersecurity* was created to address this shift.

This book is intentionally designed as a two-part learning system:

**Part I** focuses on clear, structured, exam-aligned text content, covering CompTIA Security+ objectives in a traditional, instructor-tested format.

**Part II** extends learning through *AI-enhanced prompts*, enabling readers to actively generate their own explanations, summaries, visuals, and learning artifacts.

Rather than replacing learning, AI is used in this book as a guided educational partner. Carefully crafted prompts help learners:

- Reinforce complex concepts
- Create visual representations of security topics
- Build personalized study materials
- Translate theory into practical understanding

This approach empowers learners to become active participants in their education rather than passive readers.

Whether you are preparing for the Security+ exam, learning or teaching cybersecurity, or transitioning into the field, this book encourages you to *learn deeply, visualize clearly, and apply responsibly*—the hallmarks of effective cybersecurity professionals.

**— Professor Ifti**

# How to Use This Book

This book is built as a modular, AI-enhanced learning framework. You may follow it sequentially or adapt it to your individual or instructional needs.

**Book Structure Overview**

Part I – Core Knowledge (Text-Only)

Part I delivers foundational cybersecurity concepts aligned directly with CompTIA Security+ exam objectives. This section emphasizes:

- Clear explanations
- Real-world examples
- Exam mindset guidance
- Conceptual understanding over memorization

This part can be used *independently* as a traditional Security+ textbook.

Part II – AI-Enhanced Learning & Visualization

Part II transforms learning from passive reading into active creation.

This section includes carefully designed AI prompts that guide learners to:

- Summarize topics in their own words
- Generate practice questions and explanations
- Create custom learning activities
- Design infographics for complex security concepts
- Visualize architectures, threats, and controls

These prompts are optional but highly recommended for deeper mastery.

**For Exam Candidates (Self-Study Path)**

1. Study Part I chapter by chapter
2. Identify challenging topics
3. Use corresponding Part II AI prompts to:
    - Simplify concepts
    - Create visuals
    - Test understanding

4. Revisit Part I to reinforce weak areas

*Goal:* Exam readiness with long-term understanding

**For Students in Academic or Workforce Programs**

- Instructors may assign:
    - Part I for reading
    - Part II for labs, projects, or discussions
- Students can submit:
    - AI-generated infographics
    - Concept summaries
    - Scenario explanations
- Encourages critical thinking and creativity

**For Instructors and Trainers**

This book supports blended learning and AI-assisted pedagogy.

Use Part II to:

- Design active learning exercises
- Encourage ethical AI usage
- Promote student-created content
- Replace static assignments with dynamic projects

Instructor Editions may include:

- Sample outputs
- Grading rubrics
- Classroom integration tips

**Creating Infographics with AI**

Part II includes prompts that help learners generate:

- CIA Triad diagrams
- Network security architectures
- Threat actor models
- Incident response workflows
- Risk calculation visuals

*Why this matters:* Visual learning improves retention and comprehension—especially for complex cybersecurity topics.

**Responsible Use of AI**

AI prompts in this book are designed to:

- Support learning, not replace effort
- Encourage original thinking
- Promote ethical and responsible use

Learners are expected to:

- Review AI output critically
- Verify accuracy
- Apply concepts thoughtfully

**Who Should Use Part II?**

- Students who want a deeper understanding
- Visual learners
- Instructors seeking innovation
- Professionals refreshing skills
- Anyone who learns best by creating, not just reading

**Final Guidance**

- Start with *knowledge*.
- Deepen with *creation*.
- Master through *application*.

Cybersecurity professionals are not defined by tools, but by how they *think, analyze, and adapt.*

# Ethical AI Usage Disclaimer

This book incorporates artificial intelligence (AI)–enhanced prompts to support learning, creativity, and comprehension. These prompts are provided as educational tools designed to assist learners in exploring cybersecurity concepts more effectively—not as substitutes for independent thinking, professional judgment, or hands-on experience.

Readers are expected to use AI responsibly and ethically.

**All AI-generated outputs should be:**

- Critically evaluated for accuracy and relevance
- Verified against trusted cybersecurity standards and sources
- Adapted and refined using the learner's own understanding

AI tools may produce incomplete, outdated, or inaccurate information. Therefore, learners must not rely solely on AI-generated content for exam preparation, professional decision-making, or real-world security implementations.

**The use of AI in this book is intended to:**

- Enhance understanding, not bypass learning
- Encourage ethical and transparent use of technology
- Support creativity, visualization, and problem-solving
- Promote accountability and academic integrity

**Users are responsible for complying with:**

- Institutional academic integrity policies
- Professional codes of conduct
- Applicable laws, regulations, and ethical standards

The author does not assume responsibility for misuse, misinterpretation, or overreliance on AI-generated content. All cybersecurity practices and decisions remain the responsibility of the learner or professional applying them.

By using the AI-enhanced components of this book, readers acknowledge their responsibility to apply AI thoughtfully, ethically, and in alignment with best practices in cybersecurity and education.

# Part I – Core Knowledge (Text-Only)

Part I delivers *foundational cybersecurity concepts* aligned directly with CompTIA Security+ exam objectives. This section emphasizes:

- Clear explanations
- Real-world examples
- Exam mindset guidance
- Conceptual understanding over memorization

This part can be used independently as a traditional Security+ textbook.

# Domain 1:
# General Security Concepts

# Chapter 1 – Security Controls: Your Cybersecurity Toolkit

## Exam Objective 1.1: Compare and Contrast Various Types of Security Controls

*Chapter Introduction*

Welcome to your first real cybersecurity mindset shift. Forget the Hollywood hacker tropes—real security isn't just about firewalls and encryption. It's about creating layers of protection that work together like a well-coordinated team. Think of it like securing your phone: you have a passcode (technical control), you set rules about which apps can access your location (managerial control), and you physically keep it in your pocket (physical control). In this chapter, we'll break down CompTIA's framework for categorizing ALL security measures—from policies to padlocks to software—so you can understand how organizations build defense-in-depth. This isn't just theory; it's the fundamental language you'll use to analyze every security scenario on the exam.

**Security+ Exam Mindset**

For Objective 1.1, CompTIA wants you to do two things: categorize a control (Is it technical, managerial, operational, or physical?) AND identify its type (Is it preventive, detective, etc.?). Expect scenario questions like: *"After a security breach, the company implemented biometric door readers to the server room. Which control category and type does this represent?"* You'll need to select TWO correct answers. They're testing your ability to think in this dual-layered framework.

## Section 1: Control Categories – The "What" and "Who"

**Technical Controls (The Digital Enforcers)**

**Definition**

Controls implemented through technology—hardware, software, or firmware—that automatically enforce security. They don't require human intervention to work.

**Why It Matters**

Technical controls are your automated frontline defenders. They operate at machine speed, 24/7, and are essential for protecting data in our digital world. When configured correctly, they provide consistent, reliable protection against common threats.

**Real-World Examples**

- Firewalls filtering network traffic
- Antivirus software scanning for malware
- Encryption scrambling data so only authorized parties can read it
- Access control lists (ACLs) determining who can access which files
- Intrusion Prevention Systems (IPS) blocking malicious activity in real-time

**Exam Clue**

If a control involves **software, hardware, or automated systems**, it's technical. Keywords: *automated, software-based, electronic, enforced by a system.*

**Managerial Controls (The Rule Makers)**

**Definition**

Controls focused on governance, policy, and oversight. These are the "paperwork" controls that define how security should be implemented and managed.

**Why It Matters**

Without managerial controls, technical controls would be a chaotic mess. These controls create the framework—the rules, expectations, and accountability—that guide everything else. They ensure security aligns with business goals and legal requirements.

**Real-World Examples**

- Security policies and procedures (Acceptable Use Policy, Password Policy)
- Risk assessments identifying what needs protection
- Security awareness training programs for employees
- Background checks during hiring
- Third-party risk management processes

**Exam Clue**

Think plans, policies, assessments, and training. If it's about creating rules, assessing risk, or governing processes, it's managerial.

**Operational Controls (The Day-to-Day Doers)**

**Definition**

Controls carried out by people in their daily operations to implement and maintain security. These are the human actions that bring policies to life.

**Why It Matters**

Policies don't enforce themselves. Operational controls are where the rubber meets the road—where employees actually *do* the security things. Even the best technical controls fail if people don't operate them properly.

**Real-World Examples**

- User access reviews (managers periodically verifying their team's access rights)
- Backup verification (actually testing that backups can be restored)
- Incident response procedures being executed
- Configuration management following change control processes
- Media destruction (physically shredding documents or degaussing drives)

**Exam Clue**

If the scenario describes people performing specific security tasks or procedures, it's operational. Keywords: *performed by personnel, day-to-day activities, implementation of policies.*

**Physical Controls (The Tangible Barriers)**

**Definition**

Controls that protect facilities, hardware, and personnel through physical measures. Anything you can touch that provides security.

**Why It Matters**

Attackers can bypass the fanciest digital security if they can physically walk off with a server or plug into a network jack in an empty conference room. Physical controls protect the actual assets that run your technical controls.

**Real-World Examples**

- Security guards at entrances
- Mantraps (two-door entry systems)
- Badge readers on doors
- Surveillance cameras
- Locked server racks, cable locks for laptops
- Fire suppression systems in data centers

**Exam Clue**

If you can physically touch, see, or interact with it in the real world, it's a physical control. Keywords: *gates, locks, guards, cameras, environmental controls.*

## Section 2: Control Types – The "How" and "Why"

**Preventive Controls (The Stop Sign)**

**Definition**

Controls designed to stop a security incident from occurring in the first place.

**Why It Matters**

Prevention is ideal—it's cheaper, less disruptive, and protects your reputation. These controls aim to eliminate vulnerabilities or block attack vectors before they can be exploited.

**Real-World Examples**

- Firewall rules blocking malicious traffic
- Access controls preventing unauthorized users from accessing resources
- Security awareness training preventing phishing success
- Encryption preventing data exposure if stolen
- Fences and locked doors preventing physical access

**Exam Clue**

Preventive controls **stop bad things from happening**. They're proactive barriers.

**Deterrent Controls (The Warning Sign)**

**Definition**

Controls designed to discourage potential attackers by making an attack seem too difficult, risky, or unrewarding.

**Why It Matters**

Not all attackers are equally determined. Deterrent controls work on the psychology of potential threats, convincing casual or opportunistic attackers to move on to an easier target.

**Real-World Examples**

- "Warning: Surveillance in Use" signs
- Security guard presence in a lobby
- Publicized penalties for policy violations
- Well-lit parking lots at night

- Login banners stating "Unauthorized access prohibited"

**Exam Clue**

Deterrent controls don't physically stop an attack—they discourage it through perception. Key difference from preventive: a preventive lock *stops* entry; a deterrent sign *warns* against trying.

**Detective Controls (The Alarm System)**

**Definition**

Controls designed to identify and alert about security incidents *as they occur or after they happen.*

**Why It Matters**

You can't prevent everything. Detective controls provide visibility, so you know when a breach occurs, how it happened, and what was affected. This is crucial for minimizing damage and improving future prevention.

**Real-World Examples**

- Intrusion Detection Systems (IDS) alerting on suspicious traffic
- Security cameras recording activity
- Log monitoring and SIEM systems correlating events
- Antivirus software detecting malware infections
- Motion sensors triggering alarms

**Exam Clue**

Detective controls *identify, log, and alert*. They don't stop the action—they tell you it's happening or happened.

**Corrective Controls (The Cleanup Crew)**

**Definition**

Controls implemented *after* an incident to limit damage, restore systems, and prevent recurrence.

**Why It Matters**

When prevention and detection fail, correction minimizes business impact. These controls help recover from incidents and fix the vulnerabilities that were exploited.

**Real-World Examples**

- Restoring data from backups after a ransomware attack
- Patching a system after it was exploited
- Isolating or removing malware from infected systems
- Hot sites for business continuity after a disaster
- Incident response teams containing a breach

**Exam Clue**

Corrective controls come into play *after* an incident. Keywords: *restore, recover, fix, patch, contain.*

**Compensating Controls (The Plan B)**

**Definition**

Alternative controls are implemented when a primary control isn't feasible, is too expensive, or is temporarily unavailable.

**Why It Matters**

In the real world, perfect security isn't always possible. Compensating controls provide a reasonable alternative that still manages risk to an acceptable level when the ideal solution can't be used.

**Real-World Examples**

- Using two-person integrity (requiring two people to perform a sensitive task) when dual-control systems aren't available
- Implementing additional logging and monitoring when a critical patch can't be applied immediately
- Using manual review processes where automated controls would be ideal, but too costly
- Temporary security guards while an electronic access system is being repaired

**Exam Clue**

Compensating controls are alternatives that address the same risk as a primary control that can't be used. Look for scenarios where the "ideal" control isn't in place, but something else fills the gap.

**Directive Controls (The Instruction Manual)**

**Definition**

Controls that direct, confine, or guide human behavior to comply with security policies.

**Why It Matters**

People need to know what's expected of them. Directive controls communicate requirements and ensure everyone understands their security responsibilities.

**Real-World Examples**

- Policies, standards, and guidelines telling employees what to do
- Signed agreements (acceptable use policies, NDAs)
- Posted instructions for secure procedures
- Legal and regulatory requirements (GDPR, HIPAA) mandating certain protections

**Exam Clue**

Directive controls tell people what to do. They're about communication, guidance, and formal requirements.

# Chapter Summary

Think of security controls as your complete cybersecurity toolkit. First, you categorize them by *implementation method* (Technical, Managerial, Operational, Physical)—is it a tech tool, a policy, a human action, or a physical barrier? Then you identify their purpose type (Preventive, Deterrent, Detective, Corrective, Compensating, Directive)—does it stop, discourage, detect, fix, substitute, or guide?

Remember: One control can fit multiple categories and types. A firewall is both Technical (category) and Preventive (type). Security cameras are Physical (category) and both Detective (record incidents) and Deterrent (visible presence warns people).

**Exam-Related Tips**

1. Two-Part Thinking: Always ask: (1) What kind of control is this? (Category) AND (2) What does it do? (Type)
2. Scenario Analysis: Exam questions will describe a situation. Read carefully—is the control being implemented *before, during,* or *after* an incident? That tells you the type.
3. Managerial vs. Operational: Managerial = creating the rules. Operational = carrying out the rules.
4. Deterrent vs. Preventive: If it physically stops the action = Preventive. If it just makes someone think twice = Deterrent.

**Think Like the Exam**

Question: *"Following a data breach where an employee fell for a phishing scam, the company now requires all employees to complete quarterly security awareness training. The training includes simulated phishing emails. Which TWO control types are implemented?"*

Break it down:

- The requirement to complete training is a Directive control (it directs behavior).
- The simulated phishing emails are a Preventive control (they aim to prevent future incidents by teaching detection).

The category? The training program itself is Managerial (governance), but employees taking it are Operational (people carrying out procedures). The question asks for *types*, not categories, so Directive and Preventive are correct.

**Self-Reflection Prompt**

Look around your workspace right now—physical or digital. Identify three security controls you can see. For each, try to categorize it (Technical/Managerial/Operational/Physical) AND type it (Preventive/Deterrent/etc). For example: Your laptop password = Technical + Preventive. A "Clean Desk Policy" sign = Directive + (arguably) Deterrent. This exercise builds the mental muscle memory for the exam.

# Chapter 2 – The Security Foundation: CIA, AAA, and Beyond

## Exam Objective 1.2:

## Summarize fundamental security concepts

*Chapter Introduction*

Welcome to security's rulebook. Before you can configure a firewall or analyze a log, you need to understand WHY we do any of this. What are we actually protecting? In this chapter, we'll break down the core principles that guide every security decision—from protecting your Instagram DMs to securing a national power grid. We're covering the legendary CIA Triad, the gatekeeping AAA framework, the modern Zero Trust mindset, and the physical/digital tricks that keep attackers guessing. This isn't just theory; this is the DNA of cybersecurity. Master these concepts, and you'll understand the purpose behind every tool and policy you'll encounter on the exam and in the real world.

**Security+ Exam Mindset**

For Objective 1.2, CompTIA is testing your vocabulary and conceptual understanding. You must not only define these terms but also apply them to scenarios. Expect questions that present a situation (e.g., "An attacker alters transaction logs") and ask which principle was violated. Or they'll describe a security architecture and ask which fundamental concept it represents. This objective is about speaking the native language of cybersecurity fluently.

## Section 1: The CIA Triad – Security's Three Pillars

**Confidentiality, Integrity, and Availability (CIA)**

**Definition**

The foundational model of information security:

- **Confidentiality:** Keeping data private and unseen by unauthorized people. "Who should see this?"
- **Integrity:** Ensuring data is accurate, trustworthy, and unaltered. "Can I trust this hasn't been changed?"

- **Availability:** Ensuring data and systems are accessible to authorized users when needed. "Can I get to it when I need it?"

**Why It Matters**

Every single security control you'll ever encounter exists to support one or more of these three goals. They often exist in tension—strong encryption (confidentiality) can slow system access (availability). Security is about balancing all three based on what you're protecting.

**Real-World Example**

- **Online Banking:**
  - **Confidentiality:** Your account balance is encrypted and hidden behind login credentials.
  - **Integrity:** The system ensures your $100 transfer stays $100 and isn't altered to $1000 mid-transaction.
  - **Availability:** The bank's website and app need to be up 24/7 for you to access your money.

**Exam Clue**

- **Confidentiality = Secrecy/Privacy.**
  Keywords: *encryption, access controls, steganography.*
- **Integrity = Trustworthiness/Accuracy.**
  Keywords: *hashing, digital signatures, checksums, change management.*
- **Availability = Uptime/Access.**
  Keywords: *redundancy, backups, fault tolerance, DDoS protection.*

## Section 2: Proving It Happened & Who Did It

**Non-repudiation**

**Definition**

The ability to prevent a person or system from denying (repudiating) the truth of an action they took, particularly in a digital transaction. It provides undeniable proof of origin and integrity.

**Why It Matters**

Imagine sending a "fire" email to your boss and then saying, "That wasn't me!" Non-repudiation ensures accountability in digital spaces, which is critical for legal evidence, financial transactions, and system audits.

**Real-World Example**

When you digitally sign a PDF with a certificate from a trusted authority (like DocuSign), you're using non-repudiation. The cryptographic signature uniquely ties that document to you and proves it hasn't been altered since you signed it. You cannot later deny having signed it.

**Exam Clue**

Non-repudiation is about undeniable proof. It's often achieved through digital signatures and comprehensive audit logging. If a question is about proving who sent a message or took an action, think non-repudiation.

## Section 3: The Gatekeeper's Playbook: AAA

**Authentication, Authorization, and Accounting (AAA)**

**Definition**

The three-step process for controlling access to resources:

1. **Authentication (AuthN):** Verifying *who* you are. "Are you who you say you are?"
2. **Authorization (AuthZ):** Determining *what* you're allowed to do. "Now that I know who you are, what are you allowed to access?"
3. **Accounting (Auditing):** Tracking *what* you did. "What actions did you take while logged in?"

**Why It Matters**

AAA is the sequential process for every access decision. Getting the order wrong breaks security. You must authenticate *before* you authorize, and you must log (account) for accountability and investigation.

**Real-World Example – Entering a Secure Office Building:**

1. **Authentication:** You badge in at the front door (something you have).
2. **Authorization:** Your badge grants you access to the 3rd floor (your office) but not the 5th floor (executive suite).
3. **Accounting:** The security system logs your name, time of entry, and door used.

**Authenticating People vs. Systems**

- **Authenticating People:** Uses factors like passwords (something you know), smart cards (something you have), and fingerprints (something you are).

- **Authenticating Systems (Machine AuthN):** Uses digital certificates, API keys, or pre-shared keys to allow servers, IoT devices, or applications to prove their identity to each other automatically.

**Authorization Models**

**Why It Matters**

Once authenticated, the system needs a rulebook to decide your privileges.

- **Mandatory Access Control (MAC):** Strict, labels-based. Used by governments/military. The *system* (based on security labels like "Top Secret") decides what you can access. You, as a user, cannot change this.
- **Discretionary Access Control (DAC):** Flexible, user-based. The *owner* of a resource (like a file) decides who can access it. Think of file permissions on your laptop.
- **Role-Based Access Control (RBAC):** Efficient, business-based. Access is based on your *job role* (e.g., "Accountant," "HR Manager"). Add a user to the "Accountant" group, and they get all permissions for that role.
- **Attribute-Based Access Control (ABAC):** Dynamic, context-based. Access decisions are based on multiple attributes (user's department, time of day, location, device security posture). The most granular model.

**Exam Clue**

- **MAC = "Military."** Labels, system-controlled, most restrictive.
- **DAC = "Discretion."** User/owner-controlled.
- **RBAC = "Role."** Group/Job-title based.
- **ABAC = "Attributes."** "If-then" policies using multiple factors.

## Section 4: Planning and the New Mindset

**Gap Analysis**

**Definition**

A methodical comparison of an organization's *current* security state against a *desired* future state (like a compliance standard or best-practice framework) to identify deficiencies ("gaps").

**Why It Matters**

You can't fix what you don't know is broken. Gap analysis is the first step in any security improvement plan. It provides a roadmap by asking, "Where are we now, where do we need to be, and what's missing to get there?"

**Real-World Example**

A healthcare clinic needs to comply with HIPAA. They perform a gap analysis by checking their current controls against the HIPAA Security Rule checklist. They discover they encrypt data at rest (good), but lack a formal incident response plan (gap). This finding directs their resources to develop that plan.

**Zero Trust**

**Definition**

A security model based on the principle of "never trust, always verify." It assumes no user or device—inside or outside the network—is trustworthy by default. Every access request must be authenticated, authorized, and encrypted.

**Why The Old Model Failed:** The traditional "castle-and-moat" approach trusted anyone inside the network. Once an attacker breached the perimeter (the moat), they could move freely (inside the castle). Zero Trust eliminates this concept of a trusted internal network.

**Real-World Analogy**

An exclusive club with a bouncer at every interior door, not just the front entrance. Getting past the front door doesn't grant you access to the VIP lounge, the back office, or the storage room. Each door requires re-verification of your credentials.

**Zero Trust Components:**

- **Control Plane (The Brain):** Where access decisions are made.
    - **Adaptive Identity:** Continuously re-assessing user/device risk based on behavior (e.g., logging in from a new country triggers MFA).
    - **Threat Scope Reduction:** Minimizing attack surface by segmenting networks and granting least-privilege access.
    - **Policy-Driven Access Control:** Dynamic policies (like ABAC) that govern access.
    - **Policy Administrator & Policy Engine:** The systems that create, manage, and enforce the access policies.
- **Data Plane (The Muscle):** Where policies are enforced.
    - **Implicit Trust Zones:** Micro-segments of the network. Nothing is trusted by default.
    - **Subject/System:** The user or device requesting access.

- **Policy Enforcement Point (PEP):** The gateway (like a firewall or proxy) that actually allows or blocks the access request based on instructions from the Control Plane.

**Exam Clue**

Zero Trust is a huge exam theme. Key phrases: *"never trust, always verify," "assume breach," "least privilege," "micro-segmentation."* Understand that it applies to *all* traffic, internal and external.

## Section 5: The Physical World

**Physical Security Controls**

**Definition**

Tangible measures to protect people, hardware, and facilities.

**Why It Matters**

The most advanced cybersecurity is useless if someone can walk into a server room and unplug a machine or steal a hard drive. Physical security is the first layer of defense.

**Real-World Examples & Purpose:**

- **Bollards:** Short, sturdy posts to prevent vehicle ramming attacks.
- **Access Control Vestibule (Mantrap):** A two-door entry system preventing tailgating; only one door opens at a time.
- **Fencing:** Establishes a perimeter. Delay control type.
- **Video Surveillance (CCTV):** Detective and Deterrent controls.
- **Security Guard:** Deterrent, Detective, and Corrective (can respond).
- **Access Badge:** Preventive and Physical/Technical control.
- **Lighting:** A Deterrent control to discourage clandestine activity.
- **Sensors:**
  - Infrared: Detects heat/movement.
  - Pressure: Detects weight on a floor or mat.
  - Microwave/Ultrasonic: Fills a space with waves; disturbances signal intrusion.

## Section 6: Playing Mind Games with Attackers

### Deception and Disruption Technology

#### Definition

Security tools designed to mislead, detect, or waste an attacker's time by presenting fake, attractive targets.

#### Why It Matters

These are proactive, detective controls. They turn the tables by making attackers reveal themselves while interacting with worthless decoys, allowing defenders to study their tactics and gather threat intelligence.

#### Real-World Examples:

- **Honeypot:** A single, isolated decoy system (server, database) designed to lure attackers.
- **Honeynet:** A network of multiple honeypots, simulating a more realistic environment.
- **Honeyfile:** A fake, tempting file (e.g., "passwords.txt") that alerts admins when accessed.
- **Honeytoken:** A fake piece of data (a fake database entry, API key, or credit card number) that triggers an alert if used.

#### Exam Clue

Deception tech is always for detection and intelligence gathering, not primary prevention. If an exam question mentions a fake server set up to monitor attacker behavior, it's describing a honeypot.

# Chapter Summary

You've now built your security vocabulary foundation. The CIA Triad (Confidentiality, Integrity, Availability) defines our goals. AAA (Authentication, Authorization, Accounting) defines our access control process. Non-repudiation provides legal-grade proof. Gap analysis finds our weaknesses. Zero Trust is the modern "verify everything" architecture that replaces the old "trusted internal network" model. Physical security protects the tangible assets, and deception technology (honeypots/files/tokens) turns attackers into our intelligence source.

**Exam-Related Tips**

1. **CIA Scenarios:** Read carefully. "Data was modified" = Integrity breach. "Data was leaked" = Confidentiality breach. "Website is down" = Availability breach.
2. **AAA Order is Sacred:** Authentication → Authorization → Accounting. Never changes.
3. **Zero Trust is Everywhere:** Expect multiple questions. Remember its core tenets: least privilege, micro-segmentation, explicit verification.
4. **Deception = Detection:** Honeypots are for learning about attacks, not stopping them initially.

**Think Like the Exam**

*Question: "A company deploys a server configured with weak passwords and fake financial records. Security analysts monitor all traffic to this server. Which security concept does this BEST represent, and what is the primary purpose?"*

- It's not a primary production server (so not a core availability issue).
- It's designed to attract and study attackers.
- This is a classic Honeypot (Deception Technology). Its primary purpose is detection and threat intelligence gathering.

**Self-Reflection Prompt**

Pick an app on your phone. How does it implement the CIA Triad for your data? How does it handle AAA when you log in? Now, imagine how a Zero Trust model would change your experience with that app (hint: more frequent re-checks, stricter access rules). This connects abstract concepts to your daily tech life.

# Chapter 3 – Managing Change: The Art of Not Breaking Things

## Exam Objective 1.3: Explain the importance of change management processes and the impact to security

*Chapter Introduction*

Picture this: It's 2 AM. A system admin, fueled by caffeine, pushes a "quick fix" to a live server to solve a minor bug. Suddenly, the entire company's payment system goes down. Revenue stops. Panic ensues. This isn't a hacker attack—it's unmanaged change, the silent killer of security and stability. In this chapter, we'll explore why cybersecurity isn't just about fighting external threats; it's about controlling the chaos *inside* your own systems. Change management is the formal process that turns risky, off-the-cuff tweaks into predictable, safe improvements. For the Security+ exam, you need to understand that how you manage a software update is just as critical as the firewall rule that the update might contain.

**Security+ Exam Mindset**

CompTIA views change management as a core security function. You won't be asked to memorize a specific vendor's process, but you must understand the universal *phases, components, and security implications* of any change management workflow. Expect scenario questions that ask, "*Which step was missed?*" when a change causes an outage, or "*What is the primary security purpose of a backout plan?*" Think of this as learning the rules of the road to prevent internal security crashes.

## Section 1: The Business Process – Getting Permission to Change

Change management is a structured business process. It's about getting the right people to say "yes" for the right reasons, before you touch anything.

**Approval Process**

**Definition**

The formal workflow where a proposed change is reviewed and authorized by designated personnel (like a Change Advisory Board or manager) before implementation.

**Why It Matters for Security**

Approval prevents unilateral, risky decisions. It ensures someone with a broader view of business risk assesses the security impact. An unapproved change is, by definition, unauthorized and a potential security incident.

**Real-World Example**

A developer cannot directly patch a production database. They must submit a change request ticket detailing the patch, its source, and the tested fix. The security team reviews it for vulnerabilities, the database team reviews it for performance, and the CAB approves it for a scheduled maintenance window.

**Ownership & Stakeholders**

- **Ownership:** Clearly identifying who is ultimately responsible for the system being changed and for executing the change itself. No change should be "everyone's problem."
- **Stakeholders:** All parties affected by the change (security team, network team, compliance, business units).

**Why It Matters for Security**

Clear ownership ensures accountability. Identifying stakeholders means the security team—a key stakeholder—always gets a seat at the table to assess risk, preventing changes that weaken the security posture.

**Impact Analysis**

**Definition**

The step where the change proposer predicts the effects of the change on systems, performance, security, and users.

**Why It Matters for Security**

This is where you ask the critical security question: "*What could break or become vulnerable?*" For example, applying an OS patch might impact a legacy, business-critical application that the security team wasn't aware of, creating a denial-of-service.

**Exam Clue**

A question describing a change that unexpectedly took down a related service is highlighting a failed or missing impact analysis.

**Test Results & Backout Plan**

- **Test Results:** Evidence from a staging environment that proves the change works as intended and doesn't introduce new vulnerabilities.
- **Backout Plan (Rollback Plan):** A predefined, tested procedure to quickly revert the change and restore the system to its previous state if something goes wrong.

**Why It Matters for Security**

Testing is where you find security flaws *before* production. The backout plan is a corrective control for security. If a patch introduces a critical vulnerability, the backout plan is your emergency response to immediately reduce risk.

**Real-World Example**

Before deploying a new firewall rule, you test it in a lab. The test shows the rule also accidentally blocks IT management traffic—a security and operational problem. You fix the rule *before* deployment. The backout plan is simply to disable the new rule, reverting to the old configuration.

**Maintenance Window**

**Definition**

A scheduled, often off-peak time period during which changes can be implemented, minimizing disruption to users and business operations.

**Why It Matters for Security**

Implementing changes during low-activity periods gives you time to monitor for security anomalies post-change and execute the backout plan calmly if needed, without the pressure of peak business traffic.

**Standard Operating Procedure (SOP)**

**Definition**

The formal, documented steps that must be followed to execute a specific type of change.

**Why It Matters for Security**

SOPs enforce consistency and ensure security steps (like pre- and post-change vulnerability scans) are never skipped. They turn best practices into a mandatory routine.

## Section 2: The Technical Reality – What Actually Changes

Once the business side approves, you face the technical execution. This is where security meets the metal.

**Allow Lists / Deny Lists**

**Definition**

- **Allow List (Formerly Whitelist):** A security model that permits *only* explicitly pre-approved applications, network traffic, or users. Default is DENY.
- **Deny List (Formerly Blacklist):** A model that blocks known-bad entities. Default is ALLOW.

**Why Change Management Matters Here**

Adding an entry to an allow list is a high-risk change. You are explicitly creating a new permitted pathway. This *must* go through rigorous change control with strong justification and security review to avoid creating a backdoor.

**Exam Clue**

CompTIA emphasizes Allow Listing as the more secure model. A change to an allow list is more critical than one to a deny list.

**Restricted Activities & Dependencies**

- **Restricted Activities:** Actions that are high-risk and often prohibited during certain hours or without special approval (e.g., changing firewall rules, disabling security software).
- **Dependencies:** Other systems or services that rely on the system being changed.

**Why It Matters for Security**

A change that seems isolated (updating a library) can break a dependency (an app that uses that library), causing downtime or disabling security controls. Change management forces the mapping of these dependencies.

**Downtime, Service Restart, Application Restart**

**Definition**

The expected or unexpected unavailability of a system or function due to the change.

**Why It Matters for Security**

**Downtime is an availability (CIA Triad) impact.** From a security perspective, restarts can also be risky: when a service restarts, its security settings and connections are re-established—a moment where misconfigurations can cause failures or where temporary security bypasses might be exposed.

**Legacy Applications**

**Definition**

Older software that is critical to business operations but may be unsupported, unable to run on modern OSes, or incompatible with current security controls.

**Why Change Management is CRITICAL Here**

Changing *anything* in an environment with a legacy app is like performing surgery near a bomb. An OS patch, a network setting change, or a security update could render the legacy app inoperable. Change management for legacy systems requires extreme impact analysis, testing, and often a parallel support plan.

## Section 3: Documentation – The Memory of Your Network

If it isn't documented, it doesn't exist. Documentation is a managerial security control.

**Updating Diagrams & Policies/Procedures**

- **Diagrams:** Network diagrams, data flow diagrams, system architecture maps.
- **Policies/Procedures:** Security policies, runbooks, SOPs.

**Why It Matters for Security**

An outdated network diagram during an incident response is a disaster. You can't secure what you don't know you have. Version control (tracking changes to documents) is part of this. It ensures everyone is working from the correct, latest set of "blueprints" and prevents accidental reversion to an insecure configuration.

**Real-World Example**

You add a new server to the DMZ. If you don't update the network diagram, the firewall admin might not know to create specific rules for it, leaving it overexposed. If you don't update the asset inventory, the vulnerability scanner won't scan it, leaving it unpatched.

# Chapter Summary

Change management is the disciplined heartbeat of a secure organization. The business process (approval, impact analysis, backout planning) ensures risks are evaluated and authorized. The technical implementation (handling allow lists, dependencies, restarts) is where those risks become real, especially for fragile legacy systems. Finally, documentation (updated diagrams, version-controlled policies) closes the loop, ensuring your organization's knowledge stays current and actionable. Security isn't a one-time state; it's a property maintained through careful, controlled evolution.

**Exam-Related Tips**

1. **Backout Plan is Key:** It's your safety net. On the exam, if a change fails and there's chaos, the missing step is often a **tested backout plan**.
2. **Security is a Stakeholder:** In any change management scenario, the security team must be involved to assess risk.
3. **Legacy = Danger:** Any change involving a legacy application implies high risk and requires extensive testing.
4. **Allow List > Deny List:** Understand that modifying an allow list is a more security-sensitive change than modifying a deny list.

**Think Like the Exam**

*Question: "After a scheduled patch deployment, a critical accounting application fails. The IT team works frantically for hours to restore service. Which change management component, if properly implemented, would have most likely minimized this disruption?"*

- The patch was scheduled, so approval and a window might have existed.
- The app failed *after* deployment.
- The team scrambled *without* a clear path back.
- The correct answer focuses on the Backout Plan. A tested rollback procedure would have restored the old, working state in minutes, minimizing downtime while a fix was found.

**Self-Reflection Prompt**

Think of the last time an app on your phone or computer updated automatically. Now, imagine you're the change manager for that company. What are 2-3 security risks that update could have introduced? What tests would you want to see before approving it? What would your backout plan be if the update bricked people's devices? This shifts your perspective from user to defender.

# Domain 2:
# Threats, Vulnerabilities, and Mitigations

# Chapter 4 – Cryptography: The Math That Guards Your Digital Life

## Exam Objective 1.4:

## Explain the importance of using appropriate cryptographic solutions

*Chapter Introduction*

Imagine sending a love letter through a busy cafeteria, knowing anyone could read it. That's the internet without cryptography. Cryptography is the art and science of scrambling information so only the intended recipient can understand it. But it's so much more than just "keeping secrets"—it's about proving who you are (authentication), ensuring a message wasn't tampered with (integrity), and legally binding digital agreements (non-repudiation). In this chapter, we'll break down the toolkit—from the SSL lock icon you see every day to the blockchain tech behind cryptocurrencies. For the Security+ exam, you don't need to be a mathematician, but you *do* need to know which tool solves which security problem.

**Security+ Exam Mindset**

This objective is massive. CompTIA tests cryptography conceptually and comparatively. You must know *what* each technology does, *when* to use it, and its *strengths/weaknesses* relative to others. Expect "compare and contrast" questions: "Which provides confidentiality but not integrity?" or "What is the difference between encryption and hashing?" You'll also get scenario-based questions: "A company needs to ensure data on stolen laptops is unreadable. Which solution is BEST?"

## Section 1: The Trust Framework – Public Key Infrastructure (PKI)

**Public Key Infrastructure (PKI)**

**Definition**

The entire system of hardware, software, policies, and procedures that creates, manages, distributes, uses, stores, and revokes digital certificates and public keys. It's the "DMV" for digital identities.

**Why It Matters**

PKI enables trust between strangers on the internet. It's what allows your browser to trust that bankofamerica.com is actually Bank of America and not a fake site.

**Core Components:**

- **Public Key:** A cryptographic key that can be shared publicly. It's used to encrypt data or verify a digital signature.
- **Private Key:** A cryptographic key that is kept secret. It's used to decrypt data or create a digital signature. These two keys are mathematically linked.
- **Key Escrow:** The controversial practice of storing a copy of a private key with a trusted third party (like a government or company) for recovery purposes. It creates a backdoor—a major security vs. accessibility trade-off.

**Real-World Example (Web Browsing):**

When you connect to a secure website (https://):

1. The server sends your browser its digital certificate, which contains its public key.
2. Your browser checks if a trusted Certificate Authority (CA) signed the certificate.
3. If trusted, your browser uses the server's public key to establish a secure, encrypted session.

**Exam Clue: PKI = Trust.** It's used for SSL/TLS, digital signatures, and secure email. Remember: Public key encrypts, Private key decrypts (for confidentiality). Private key signs, Public key verifies (for integrity/authentication).

## Section 2: The Scramblers – Encryption

**Definition:** The process of converting plaintext (readable data) into ciphertext (scrambled data) using an algorithm and a key.

**Encryption Levels (What are we encrypting?)**

- **Full-Disk Encryption (FDE):** Encrypts *entire* storage drive (e.g., BitLocker, FileVault). Protects against physical theft.
- **Partition/Volume Encryption:** Encrypts a specific section of a drive.
- **File Encryption:** Encrypts individual files.
- **Database Encryption:** Can be whole database, tablespace, or column/record-level.
- **Record Encryption:** Encrypting specific rows in a database (most granular).

**Why Level Matters: FDE** is great for lost laptops, but doesn't protect data in transit over a network. File/Database encryption offers more granular control for specific sensitive data.

**Symmetric vs. Asymmetric Encryption**

- **Symmetric Encryption:** Uses the SAME key to encrypt and decrypt. (Example: AES, ChaCha20, 3DES).
    - **Pros:** *Fast* and efficient for bulk data.
    - **Cons:** Key Distribution Problem – how do you securely share the single secret key?
- **Asymmetric Encryption:** Uses a key pair (Public and Private). What one encrypts, the other decrypts. (Example: RSA, Elliptic Curve).
    - **Pros:** Solves the key distribution problem. Enables digital signatures.
    - **Cons:** *Slow*. Not practical for encrypting large amounts of data.

**Real-World Hybrid Use:** HTTPS uses asymmetric encryption to securely exchange a symmetric session key. Then, all data in that session is encrypted with the fast symmetric key. Best of both worlds.

**Key Concepts**

- **Key Exchange:** The method of securely sharing cryptographic keys. Diffie-Hellman is a famous algorithm for this, often used in TLS.
- **Algorithms & Key Length:** The mathematical formula (AES, RSA) and the size of the key (256-bit, 2048-bit). Longer key = stronger encryption, but slower. AES-256 is a symmetric standard. RSA 2048+ is an asymmetric standard.
- **Transport/Communication Encryption:** Protecting data *while it moves* (e.g., TLS for web, IPsec for VPNs, SRTP for voice).

## Section 3: The Hardware Helpers – Tools

- **Trusted Platform Module (TPM):** A dedicated microcontroller chip on a computer's motherboard that securely generates, stores, and manages cryptographic keys (e.g., for FDE like BitLocker). Protects keys from software attacks.
- **Hardware Security Module (HSM):** A dedicated, hardened, often network-connected physical device that performs crypto operations and manages keys. It is more robust than a TPM and is used by banks and Certificate Authorities (CAs).

- **Key Management System (KMS):** The software-based system (or service, like AWS KMS) for generating, distributing, rotating, and destroying cryptographic keys throughout their lifecycle.
- **Secure Enclave:** A physically isolated coprocessor within a main CPU (like in Apple Silicon) that provides an extra layer of security for sensitive data processing.

**Why Hardware Matters:** Hardware-based security raises the bar. Stealing a key from an HSM is vastly harder than stealing it from a software file on a disk.

## Section 4: The Hiders – Obfuscation

**Obfuscation**

**Definition:** Techniques that hide or disguise data, but do not provide strong cryptographic protection.

- **Steganography:** Hiding data *inside* another file (e.g., a text inside an image's pixel data). Security through obscurity.
- **Tokenization:** Replacing sensitive data (like a credit card number) with a random, non-sensitive equivalent called a "token." The real data is stored in a secure vault. Used in payment systems.
- **Data Masking:** Obscuring specific data within a database (e.g., showing only the last 4 digits of a SSN: XXX-XX-1234). Used for development/testing with real data.

**Exam Clue:** Obfuscation ≠ Encryption. If a question is about *hiding existence* (steganography) or *protecting data in non-production environments* (masking), think obfuscation. For true confidentiality against a determined attacker, you need encryption.

## Section 5: The Fingerprinters – Hashing & Salting

- **Hashing:** A one-way mathematical function that takes input (any size) and produces a fixed-length string (hash/digest). Cannot be reversed.
  - **Purpose: Integrity.** If the data changes even 1 bit, the hash changes completely (avalanche effect). Used for password storage, file verification, and blockchain.
  - **Algorithms:** SHA-256, SHA-3.
- **Salting:** Adding a random, unique string to each password *before* hashing it.
  - **Why?** Defeats rainbow table attacks (precomputed tables of hashes). Even if two users have the same password, their salts make the hashes different.

- **Key Stretching:** Deliberately slowing down the hashing process (e.g., using PBKDF2, bcrypt, Argon2) to make brute-force attacks computationally infeasible.

**Real-World Example (Password Storage):**

1. User creates password: mypass123
2. System generates a unique salt: a91!xP
3. System hashes mypass123a91!xP using key-stretching (bcrypt).
4. Stores hash + salt in the database. The plaintext password is never stored.

## Section 6: The Provers – Digital Signatures & Blockchain

- **Digital Signatures:** Provide integrity, authentication, and non-repudiation.
    - How it works: You create a hash of the message. You encrypt that hash with your private key. The recipient decrypts the signature with your public key, recomputes the message hash, and compares. If they match, the message is authentic and unaltered.
- **Blockchain:** A decentralized, distributed public ledger where transactions are recorded in blocks, cryptographically linked (hashed) to the previous block, making the chain tamper-evident.
- **Open Public Ledger:** The transparent, viewable record of all transactions in a blockchain (e.g., Bitcoin).

## Section 7: The Trust Mechanics – Certificates

- **Certificate Authorities (CA):** The trusted entities (like DigiCert, Let's Encrypt) that issue and sign digital certificates, vouching that a public key belongs to a specific identity.
- **Root of Trust:** The top-level, self-signed CA certificate embedded in your OS/browser. You inherently trust it.
- **Certificate Signing Request (CSR):** The file sent to a CA to apply for a certificate. Contains the public key and identity info.
- **Types:** Third-party (from public CA), Self-signed (you are your own CA—good for internal testing, browsers don't trust it by default), Wildcard (*.example.com covers all subdomains).
- **Revocation:** When a certificate is compromised or invalid before its expiry.
    - **Certificate Revocation List (CRL):** A CA-published list of revoked certificates. Client must download the entire list to check.

- **Online Certificate Status Protocol (OCSP):** A query protocol where a client asks the CA, "Is this certificate revoked?" in real-time. More efficient than CRL.

**Exam Clue:** OCSP vs. CRL is a common comparison. OCSP is real-time and doesn't transfer a full list, but it requires connectivity and can create privacy concerns (the CA knows what sites you're visiting).

# Chapter Summary

Choosing the appropriate cryptographic solution is a core security skill. Use encryption (symmetric/asymmetric) for *confidentiality*. Use **hashing (with salt and key stretching)* for *integrity* and password protection. Use **digital signatures/PKI* for *authentication, integrity, and non-repudiation*. Use **hardware (TPM/HSM)* to protect the keys themselves. **Obfuscation (tokenization, masking)* has specific use cases but isn't strong crypto. And the entire trust model of the web rests on certificates and CAs, managed through revocation with CRL/OCSP.

**Exam-Related Tips**

1. Symmetric = Speed, Asymmetric = Trust. Know their roles in the TLS handshake.
2. Hashing is ONE-WAY, Encryption is TWO-WAY. You can't "decrypt" a hash.
3. Salting defeats rainbow tables. Key stretching defeats brute force.
4. Digital Signature = Private key signs, Public key verifies.
5. CRL = List, OCSP = Query. OCSP is more modern but has a privacy trade-off.

**Think Like the Exam**

*Question: "A security administrator needs to protect customer credit card data stored in a database used by a payment application. The solution must allow the application to process payments without exposing the actual card numbers to the database administrators. Which combination of solutions should the administrator implement?"*

- We need to protect data *at rest* in the DB, but the app still needs to *use* it.
- Full-disk encryption would expose data to the DB admin when the DB is running.
- File/database encryption with app-managed keys is better, but the app needs the key.
- The BEST fit here is Tokenization. The real numbers are stored in a separate, ultra-secure vault. The database holds only tokens. The payment app exchanges the token for the real number via the vault's API, never exposing it to DB admins.

**Self-Reflection Prompt**

Open your browser and click the padlock icon next to the URL. View the site's certificate. Can you identify the Certificate Authority? The Public Key Algorithm? The Expiration Date? Now, think about your most used password. If the website is following best practices, what hashing algorithm and key stretching technique should they be using on it? This connects the abstract to your actual browsing.

# Chapter 5 – Know Your Enemy: Threat Actors and Their "Why"

## Exam Objective 2.1:
## Compare and contrast common threat actors and motivations

*Chapter Introduction*

Let's be real: cybersecurity isn't about fighting faceless malware. It's about understanding the people and groups behind the attacks—their skills, their resources, and most importantly, their motivations. Is it a bored teenager in a basement, a nation-state spy agency, or a disgruntled employee? Your defense strategy changes completely based on the answer. This chapter is your profile guide to the digital threat landscape. We'll build personas for each major actor, dissect their attributes, and uncover what drives them. By the end, you'll be able to look at a security incident and make an educated guess about "whodunit" and why—a critical skill for the Security+ exam and your future career.

**Security+ Exam Mindset**

CompTIA loves "compare and contrast" objectives. For 2.1, you must be able to match a described actor to their most likely motivation and attributes, and vice versa. Expect scenario questions like: "*An attack using political messages disrupts a government website. The attack uses simple DDoS tools. Which threat actor is MOST likely involved?*" You'll need to synthesize the actor, their common resources, and their typical motivation from the clues given.

## Section 1: The Cast of Characters – Threat Actors

**Nation-State**

**Definition:** Attackers sponsored by a country's government or military (e.g., APT28 "Fancy Bear" linked to Russia, APT1 linked to China).

**Why They Matter:** They are the "final boss" of threat actors. They set the bar for sophistication, patience, and impact.

**Real-World Example:** The SolarWinds supply chain attack (2020). Believed to be a nation-state operation, it compromised a trusted software update to infiltrate thousands of organizations, including US government agencies, for long-term espionage.

**Organized Crime**

**Definition:** Cybercriminal groups run like businesses, focused solely on profit. They often operate from regions with lax cyber laws.

**Why They Matter:** They are the most common financial threat to businesses. They professionalize cybercrime with customer service, R&D, and franchised attack tools.

**Real-World Example:** Ransomware-as-a-Service (RaaS) gangs like LockBit or REvil. They develop the ransomware, sell or lease it to "affiliates" who execute attacks, and split the profits. It's a franchise model for extortion.

**Hacktivist**

**Definition:** Attackers motivated by political, social, or ideological beliefs. They aim to disrupt or draw attention to a cause.

**Why They Matter:** Their goal is publicity and disruption, not stealth or direct profit. This makes their attacks noisy and often timed with real-world events.

**Real-World Example:** Anonymous operations. They might deface a corporate website, leak data, or launch DDoS attacks against organizations they oppose (e.g., governments, corporations they accuse of unethical practices).

**Insider Threat**

**Definition:** A threat that originates from within the organization. This includes malicious employees, contractors, or business partners, as well as negligent or poorly trained staff.

**Why They Matter:** They already have trust and access, bypassing most perimeter defenses. They can cause massive damage whether they intend to or not.

**Real-World Example:**

- **Malicious:** A sysadmin facing termination plants a logic bomb to delete critical data after they leave.
- **Negligent:** An employee clicks a phishing link, unknowingly installing malware that gives attackers a foothold inside the network.

**Unskilled Attacker (Script Kiddie)**

**Definition:** Individuals with little technical expertise who use pre-written scripts, tools, and exploits developed by others.

**Why They Matter:** While low in skill, they are high in volume. They often cause collateral damage while randomly scanning and attacking easy targets.

**Real-World Example:** A teenager using a simple tool like "Low Orbit Ion Cannon" to launch a DDoS attack against a school's network, not for financial gain but for personal notoriety.

**Shadow IT**

**Definition:** Not a person, but a source of risk. It refers to systems, software, or services used by employees without the approval or knowledge of the IT/security department.

**Why It Matters as a "Threat Actor":** It creates unmanaged, unsecured entry points and data leaks. Example: A sales team using an unsanctioned cloud file-sharing app to store customer data, bypassing corporate security controls.

## Section 2: Their Profile – Key Attributes

To contrast actors, we look at three key attributes:

**1. Internal vs. External**

- Internal: The actor operates from inside the organization's trust boundary. (Primary Example: Insider Threat, Shadow IT).
- External: The actor operates from the outside. (Primary Example: Nation-State, Organized Crime, Hacktivist, Unskilled Attacker).

The Exam Twist: An external actor can become an internal threat after compromising an employee's credentials or workstation.

**2. Resources/Funding**

- High Funding: Nation-states and Organized Crime. They have budgets for zero-day exploits, custom malware, and salaried developers.
- Low/No Funding: Unskilled Attackers, Hacktivists (often relying on free tools and volunteer effort).

**3. Level of Sophistication/Capability**

- High Sophistication: Nation-states (advanced persistent threats, custom tools, stealth). Organized Crime (business-like efficiency, professional malware).
- Low Sophistication: Unskilled Attackers (script usage only). Hacktivists (often use simple DDoS or defacement tools).

**The Key Insight:** Motivation often dictates sophistication. A nation-state seeking long-term espionage (motivation: espionage) needs high sophistication. A hacktivist seeking immediate publicity (motivation: disruption/chaos, philosophical beliefs) may not.

## Section 3: The "Why" – Motivations

Motivation is the engine of the attack. It dictates the target, method, and outcome.

**Data Exfiltration & Espionage**

- **Data Exfiltration:** Stealing data (PII, intellectual property, financial records).
- **Espionage:** A subset of exfiltration focused on stealing secrets for political, military, or economic advantage.
- **Most Likely Actor:** Nation-State (for military/economic espionage), Organized Crime (for PII/financial data to sell).

**Financial Gain**

- The profit motive. Includes ransom payments, stealing funds, selling stolen data, or fraud.
- **Most Likely Actor:** Organized Crime (their core business). Also Insider Threats (embezzlement).

**Service Disruption & Disruption/Chaos**

- Making systems or networks unavailable (DDoS) or otherwise disrupting operations.
- **Most Likely Actor:** Hacktivists (to make a statement), Nation-States (as a precursor to warfare or to create instability).

**Philosophical/Political Beliefs & Ethical**

- **Philosophical/Political:** Driving change or punishing an entity based on ideology.
- **Ethical:** "White hat" or vigilante actions motivated by a sense of doing good (e.g., hacking a company to expose its poor security).

- **Most Likely Actor: Hacktivists.**

**Revenge**

- Retaliation by a current or former employee, customer, or competitor.
- **Most Likely Actor:** Insider Threat (the disgruntled employee). Can also be an external actor who feels wronged.

**Blackmail/Extortion**

- Threatening to release sensitive data or cause disruption unless paid. Ransomware is a form of this.
- **Most Likely Actor:** Organized Crime.

**War**

- Cyber operations used as an extension of military conflict to disrupt critical infrastructure, communications, or command systems.
- **Sole Actor:** Nation-State.

# Chapter Summary

Think of threat intelligence as building a criminal profile. You combine the Actor (who), their Attributes (their tools and position), and their Motivation (why) to predict their behavior and tailor your defenses.

- Defending against a Nation-State (high sophistication, espionage motive) requires deep defense, advanced threat hunting, and assuming they're already inside.
- Defending against Organized Crime (financial motive, moderate-high sophistication) requires strong endpoint protection, email security, backups, and user training to stop the initial infection (often phishing).
- Defending against an Insider Threat requires strict access controls (least privilege), user behavior analytics, and a positive company culture.
- Defending against Script Kiddies is about basic cyber hygiene: patching systems, using firewalls, and disabling unused services to remove "low-hanging fruit."

**Exam-Related Tips**

1. **Connect the Dots:** Nation-State → Espionage/Foreign Intelligence. Organized Crime → Financial Gain. Hacktivist → Disruption/Philosophical Beliefs. Insider → Revenge/Financial Gain.
2. **Sophistication Scale:** Nation-State at the top, Unskilled Attacker at the bottom.
3. **Shadow IT** is a risk source, not a person. It's often the *vector* another actor exploits.
4. **"Unskilled" does not mean "harmless."** They can still cause significant damage.

**Think Like the Exam**

*Question: "A company discovers sensitive internal emails have been slowly exfiltrated over several months. The attack used a previously unknown vulnerability and custom malware that evaded signature-based detection. The data appears to have been sent to servers linked to a foreign government. Which threat actor is MOST likely responsible?"*

- **Clue 1:** "Slowly exfiltrated over several months" = patience, stealth.
- **Clue 2:** "Previously unknown vulnerability (zero-day), custom malware" = high sophistication, high resources.
- **Clue 3:** "Data sent to servers linked to a foreign government" = espionage motive.
- **Conclusion:** This profile fits only one actor: a Nation-State.

**Self-Reflection Prompt**

Think of the last major data breach you heard about in the news. Based on what was stolen and how the attack was carried out, try to profile the threat actor. What was their most likely motivation? Were they sophisticated? What does that tell you about the target's security priorities? (e.g., A fast, noisy ransomware attack suggests organized crime; a slow, quiet theft of source code suggests nation-state espionage).

# Chapter 6 – Doors and Windows: Threat Vectors & Attack Surfaces

## Exam Objective 2.2:

## Explain common threat vectors and attack surfaces

*Chapter Introduction*

You know *who* might attack you (the threat actors). Now, let's talk about *how* they get in. In cybersecurity, every point of interaction with your digital world is a potential attack surface—the doors and windows of your digital house. The threat vector is the specific path or method an attacker uses to breach that surface. Is it a malicious email? A fake website? An unpatched app? A USB stick left in the parking lot? This chapter maps out the most common ways attackers "knock" (or break in), with a special focus on social engineering—the art of hacking the human, not the machine. Mastering this is crucial for the Security+ exam, because you can't defend an entrance you don't know exists.

**Security+ Exam Mindset**

For Objective 2.2, CompTIA expects you to identify and categorize threat vectors. You'll get descriptions of attacks and need to name the vector (e.g., "An attacker calls an employee pretending to be from IT to get a password"). You also need to understand the inherent risk of different attack surfaces (like unsupported systems or open ports). Think of this as learning the toolkit of a burglar, so you know what locks to buy.

## Section 1: The Digital Delivery Vectors – How the Malware Arrives

These are the channels used to deliver a malicious payload or lure a victim.

**Message-Based (The Inbox Invaders)**

- **Email:** The #1 vector. Delivers phishing links, malware attachments (like .docm, .pdf, .zip).
- **SMS (Smishing):** Phishing via text message. "Your package delivery failed. Click here to reschedule."
- **Instant Messaging (IM):** Malicious links sent via Slack, Teams, Discord, or consumer apps.

**Image-based & File-based**

- **Image-based:** Malware hidden within image files using steganography, or malicious code in image metadata.
- **File-based:** Executable malware disguised as a legitimate document (PDF, Word, Excel) or archive file.

**Voice Call (Vishing)**

- **Definition:** "Voice phishing." Attackers call victims, often using caller ID spoofing, to impersonate trusted entities (banks, IRS, IT support) to extract information or initiate fraudulent actions.

**Removable Device**

- **Definition:** Malware that auto-runs from USB drives, external hard drives, or smartphones. An attacker might drop infected USB sticks in a company parking lot (USB baiting), counting on curiosity.

**Why These Matter:** These are the initial delivery mechanisms. Your first line of defense is filtering (email gateways) and user training ("Don't click that!").

## Section 2: The Weak Spots – Vulnerable & Unsecure Systems

These are the targets attackers aim for once they're inside or trying to get in.

**Vulnerable Software**

- **Client-based vs. Agentless:** This refers to how vulnerability scanners work, but from an attacker's view:
    - **Client-based vulnerabilities** require malware to be installed on a target (exploiting apps like browsers, Office).
    - **Agentless vulnerabilities** are exploited without pre-installed software (exploiting network services, web apps).

**Unsupported Systems & Applications**

**Definition:** Software that no longer receives security patches from the vendor (e.g., Windows 7, old versions of Java).

**Why This is Critical:** This is arguably the most dangerous attack surface. Unsupported = unpatched = publicly known vulnerabilities with *no fix*. Attackers scan specifically for these.

**Insecure Networks**

- **Wireless:** Weak encryption (WEP), open Wi-Fi hotspots, or cracked WPA2 passwords.
- **Wired:** An attacker gaining physical access to a network jack ("wall jacking").
- **Bluetooth (Bluejacking/Bluesnarfing):** Exploiting Bluetooth connections to send unsolicited messages or steal data from nearby devices.

**Open Service Ports & Default Credentials**

- **Open Service Ports:** Services like Telnet (port 23), FTP (21), or SMB (445) left open to the internet, offering attackers a direct line to attempt exploits.
- **Default Credentials:** Not changing the factory-set admin password on routers, IoT cameras, or software. Attackers use published lists of defaults.

**Real-World Example:** The Mirai botnet took over millions of IoT devices (cameras, DVRs) by scanning the internet for open Telnet/SSH ports and trying dozens of default username/password combos.

## Section 3: The Trust Betrayal – Supply Chain

**Supply Chain**

**Definition:** Attacking a target *indirectly* by first compromising a less-secure trusted partner, vendor, or service provider.

- **Managed Service Providers (MSPs):** A hacked MSP can give an attacker access to *all* the MSP's clients.
- **Vendors/Suppliers:** Compromising a software vendor to insert malware into legitimate product updates (SolarWinds attack). Or hacking a parts supplier to implant hardware backdoors.

**Why It's Devastating:** It bypasses the target's direct defenses because the attack comes from a trusted source. Defense requires vetting third-party security and monitoring for anomalous behavior even from "trusted" connections.

## Section 4: The Human Factor – Social Engineering Vectors

This is where psychology meets hacking. The goal is to manipulate people into breaking security procedures.

**Phishing & Its Variants**

- **Phishing:** Generic term for fraudulent attempts to obtain sensitive information via electronic communication.

- **Vishing:** Voice call phishing.
- **Smishing:** SMS phishing.
- **Spear Phishing:** Highly targeted phishing aimed at a specific individual or organization (more research, more convincing).
- **Whaling:** Spear phishing targeting senior executives ("big fish").

**Business Email Compromise (BEC)**

**Definition:** A sophisticated scam targeting employees who handle finances. The attacker, often after compromising an executive's email account, sends a legitimate-looking email instructing a fraudulent wire transfer. *Goal: Direct financial theft.*

**Impersonation & Pretexting**

- **Impersonation:** Pretending to be someone else (IT support, a vendor, the CEO).
- **Pretexting:** Creating a fabricated scenario (pretext) to engage a target and steal information. (e.g., "Hi, this is Gary from the bank. We're verifying unusual activity on your account. What's your mother's maiden name?").

**Watering Hole Attack**

**Definition:** Compromising a website that a specific group of people frequents. When the target visits the site, they are infected. (Like poisoning a watering hole that animals rely on).

**Brand Impersonation & Typosquatting**

- **Brand Impersonation:** Creating fake websites, social media accounts, or emails that look identical to a trusted brand.
- **Typosquatting (URL Hijacking):** Registering domains that are common misspellings of popular websites (e.g., goggle.com, amazon.com).

**Misinformation/Disinformation**

**Definition:** Spreading false or misleading information to create confusion, damage reputations, or manipulate stock prices. A modern vector for creating chaos or facilitating other scams.

# Chapter Summary

Your attack surface is the sum of all your points of exposure: your software, your network, your employees, and your partners. Threat vectors are the methods used to exploit them. The most common entry point is the human via social engineering (phishing, vishing, pretexting). The most dangerous technical weaknesses are unsupported systems and supply chain compromises. A robust defense requires layers: technical controls (patch management, email filtering, port security) and human controls (continuous security awareness training).

**Exam-Related Tips**

1. **Social Engineering is #1:** Expect multiple questions. Know the differences between Phishing, Vishing, Smishing, Spear Phishing, and Whaling.
2. **Unsupported = Unpatched = Critical Risk:** This will always be the wrong answer if you're asked for a security best practice.
3. **Supply Chain = Trusted Source:** If an attack comes from a software update or a partner, think "supply chain."
4. **Default Credentials & Open Ports** are low-hanging fruit for unskilled attackers.

**Think Like the Exam**

*Question: "An accounting department employee receives an email that appears to be from the CEO. The email states the CEO is in a meeting and needs an urgent wire transfer to close a confidential business deal. The email provides specific wire instructions. Which threat vector is being used?"*

- It's email-based.
- It's highly targeted (to the accounting department).
- The goal is direct financial fraud via a fake executive request.
- This is the classic signature of Business Email Compromise (BEC).

**Self-Reflection Prompt**

Do a quick audit of your own digital life. What's one example of a potential *attack surface* you have? (e.g., an old router, an app you haven't updated, using the same password on multiple sites). Now, what's a *threat vector* you've encountered this week? (e.g., a suspicious email, a weird text, a pop-up ad). This makes the abstract concepts personal and real.

# Chapter 7 – The Weak Points: Understanding Vulnerabilities

## Exam Objective 2.3:
## Explain various types of vulnerabilities

*Chapter Introduction*

You've met the attackers and seen their favorite entry points. Now, let's look at *what* they're actually exploiting: the *vulnerabilities*. A vulnerability is a flaw, weakness, or gap in your defenses that a threat actor can use to gain unauthorized access or cause harm. Think of it as a crack in your digital foundation. Some cracks are in the bricks (hardware), some are in the mortar (software), and some are in the blueprint itself (design). This chapter is your guide to the most critical types of vulnerabilities—from the classic buffer overflow to the modern cloud misconfigurations. For the Security+ exam, you need to recognize each type, understand how it's exploited, and know its general mitigation.

**Security+ Exam Mindset**

This objective is about categorization and comprehension. CompTIA will give you a description of a security weakness and ask you to name the type of vulnerability. You won't need to write exploit code, but you *do* need to understand the core concept behind each one (e.g., "What is a race condition?"). Expect to differentiate between similar types, like SQLi vs. XSS, or VM escape vs. resource reuse.

## Section 1: Application-Level Cracks

These are flaws in the code of software applications.

**Memory Injection & Buffer Overflow**

- **Memory Injection:** A broad category where an attacker inserts malicious code into a program's memory space to alter its execution. SQLi and XSS are forms of injection.
- **Buffer Overflow:** A specific, classic type of memory injection. It occurs when a program writes more data to a fixed-length buffer (temporary memory storage) than it can hold. The excess data "overflows" into adjacent memory, where it can overwrite instructions and allow an attacker to run their own code.

**Real-World Analogy:** Filling a glass (the buffer) with too much water. The water overflows onto the table (adjacent memory), damaging whatever is there.

**Why It Matters:** Buffer overflows have been responsible for some of the most famous exploits (e.g., Code Red, Blaster). They can give attackers full control of a system.

**Mitigation:** Input validation, secure coding practices, and compiler protections like Address Space Layout Randomization (ASLR).

**Race Conditions**

**Definition:** A flaw where the output of a process depends on the sequence/timing of uncontrollable events. The system "races" between checking a condition and acting on it.

- **Time-of-Check to Time-of-Use (TOCTTOU):**
  - **Time-of-Check (TOC):** The system checks a condition (e.g., "Does this user have permission to open this file?").
  - **Time-of-Use (TOU):** The system uses the result of that check.
  - **The Attack:** An attacker changes the condition *between* the check and the use (e.g., swapping the legitimate file with a malicious one after the permission check but before the file is opened).

**Real-World Analogy:** You check your bank balance (TOC), see $100, and decide to buy an $80 item. But before the transaction finalizes (TOU), an automatic bill payment of $50 goes through. The system now races—if the bill payment clears first, your $80 purchase should be denied.

**Mitigation:** Use *file locking* and *atomic operations* (operations that can't be interrupted) to eliminate the gap between check and use.

**Malicious Update**

**Definition:** A vulnerability introduced intentionally or via compromise into a software update. This is a primary *supply chain* attack vector.

**Why It Matters:** It abuses the trust users have in legitimate update mechanisms. Defenses like code signing aim to prevent this.

## Section 2: System & Web Vulnerabilities

**Operating System (OS)-based**

**Definition:** Flaws in the core operating system kernel or services (e.g., Windows, Linux, macOS) that can compromise the entire machine.

**Example:** A privilege escalation vulnerability that allows a standard user to gain administrator/root access.

**Web-based**

- **Structured Query Language Injection (SQLi):** Injecting malicious SQL code into a web form or parameter to manipulate the backend database. Can result in data theft, modification, or deletion.
  - **Attack String Example:** Entering ' OR '1'='1 into a login form's password field to bypass authentication.
- **Cross-Site Scripting (XSS):** Injecting malicious client-side scripts (usually JavaScript) into a web page viewed by other users. The script executes in the victim's browser, allowing session hijacking, defacement, or malware delivery.
  - **Key Difference from SQLi:** XSS targets other *users* of the website. SQLi targets the website's *database*.

**Mitigation:** Input validation & output encoding. Treat all user input as untrusted.

## Section 3: Hardware & Virtualization Flaws

**Hardware**

- **Firmware Vulnerabilities:** Flaws in the low-level software embedded in hardware (BIOS/UEFI, drive controllers, network cards). They are severe because malware can persist through OS reinstalls.
- **End-of-Life (EOL)/Legacy Hardware:** Devices no longer supported by the manufacturer. They receive no security patches for newly discovered firmware/hardware flaws.

**Virtualization**

- **Virtual Machine (VM) Escape:** An attack where code running inside a virtual machine breaks out of its isolated "guest" environment to interact with and compromise the host hypervisor. This is a catastrophic failure of isolation.
- **Resource Reuse:** A vulnerability where sensitive data is not properly wiped from memory, disk, or other resources before they are reallocated to a new VM, potentially leaking information.

## Section 4: Modern & Systemic Weaknesses

**Cloud-specific**

**Definition:** Vulnerabilities arising from the shared responsibility model and misconfiguration of cloud services (e.g., leaving an Amazon S3 storage bucket publicly readable, misconfigured identity and access management (IAM) roles).

**Why It's Common:** Cloud security is complex and often left to customers to configure. The "default to open" nature of many services creates massive attack surfaces.

**Supply Chain (Revisited)**

Vulnerabilities introduced through compromised third parties: Service, Hardware, or Software Providers. The SolarWinds attack is the textbook example of a software provider supply chain vulnerability.

**Cryptographic Vulnerabilities**

**Definition:** Weaknesses in cryptographic implementations, such as:

- Using deprecated algorithms (MD5, SHA-1, DES).
- Insufficient key length (RSA 1024-bit).
- Poor random number generation for keys.
- Implementation flaws (like the Heartbleed bug in OpenSSL).

**Misconfiguration**

**Definition:** Arguably the *#1 cause* of breaches. This is not a coding bug, but an administrative error: leaving default passwords, enabling unnecessary services, granting excessive permissions, or failing to apply security settings.

**Mobile Device Vulnerabilities**

- **Side Loading:** Installing apps from unofficial, third-party app stores, which bypass the security review of official stores (Google Play/Apple App Store).
- **Jailbreaking (iOS)/Rooting (Android):** Removing manufacturer-imposed software restrictions. This disables built-in security features (like sandboxing) and makes the device vastly more vulnerable.

## Section 5: The Ultimate Threat – Zero-day

**Zero-day**

**Definition:** A vulnerability that is unknown to the software vendor and for which there is no patch or mitigation available at the time it is discovered and exploited.

**Why It's the Most Dangerous:**

- **No Defense:** Since the vendor doesn't know about it, there are no signatures for antivirus, no patches, and no official guidance.
- **High Value:** Sold for huge sums on the black market or used by nation-states for espionage.
- **Window of Vulnerability:** Exists from the first exploit until a patch is developed, tested, and deployed (patch Tuesday).

**Mitigation Strategy:** Since you can't patch what you don't know about, defense relies on behavioral detection (EDR/XDR), network segmentation, and threat hunting.

# Chapter Summary

Vulnerabilities are the cracks attackers exploit. They exist at every layer:

- **Code Layer:** Buffer overflows, injection flaws, and race conditions.
- **System Layer:** OS flaws, web app flaws (SQLi/XSS), misconfigurations.
- **Infrastructure Layer:** Hardware/firmware, virtualization (VM escape), cloud misconfigs.
- **Process Layer:** Supply chain compromises, cryptographic weaknesses.
- **Human/Device Layer:** Mobile sideloading, jailbreaking.

The most pervasive vulnerability is misconfiguration. The most dangerous is a zero-day. Understanding these types allows you to prioritize risks: patch known bugs, harden configurations, segment networks, and implement defense-in-depth to protect against the unknowns.

**Exam-Related Tips**

1. **SQLi vs. XSS:** SQLi targets data (the database). XSS targets users (their browsers).
2. **TOCTTOU:** Remember it's about the timing gap between checking and using.
3. **Zero-day:** If a question mentions a flaw being exploited before the vendor knows about it, it's a zero-day.
4. **Misconfiguration > Coding Bugs:** More breaches happen due to bad settings than clever buffer overflows.
5. **VM Escape is a Big Deal:** It breaks the core security promise of virtualization (isolation).

**Think Like the Exam**

*Question: "A web application allows users to post comments. An attacker posts a comment that contains a script tag with malicious JavaScript. When other users view the comment page, the script executes in their browsers, stealing their session cookies. Which type of vulnerability did the attacker exploit?"*

- It's a web-based flaw.
- Malicious code is injected into a web page.
- The code executes in other users' browsers.
- This is the classic definition of a Cross-Site Scripting (XSS) vulnerability. (Not SQLi, because the database isn't the target; the users are.)

**Self-Reflection Prompt**

Think of an app or website you use. Can you guess what one of its biggest potential vulnerabilities might be, based on its function? (e.g., A social media app is a prime target for XSS. A banking app's main threat is likely misconfiguration of its cloud APIs or SQLi). This builds your ability to think like an attacker assessing a target.

# Chapter 8 – Digital Forensics 101: Spotting the Signs of an Attack

## Exam Objective 2.4:

## Given a scenario, analyze indicators of malicious activity

*Chapter Introduction*

Imagine you're a digital detective. The crime scene is a network, and the evidence is hidden in logs, system performance, and user complaints. The attackers have already slipped in. Your job isn't to stop them at the door anymore—it's to find them before they cause irreparable damage. This chapter is your guide to the indicators of compromise (IoCs)—the digital breadcrumbs, odd behaviors, and system anomalies that scream, "Something's wrong!" We'll categorize attacks by their type (malware, network, application, etc.) and, most importantly, learn the specific signs that each one leaves behind. For the Security+ exam, you'll be given a scenario packed with clues and must determine the most likely attack in progress.

**Security+ Exam Mindset**

This is a scenario-based, analytical objective. CompTIA will give you a paragraph describing symptoms—unusual network traffic, strange log entries, system performance issues, and user reports. You must connect those symptoms to a specific attack type. This tests your ability to move from observation ("CPU is at 100%") to analysis ("This indicates a crypto-mining malware infection"). Focus on the *effects* an attack has on a system or network.

### Section 1: The Infectors – Malware Attack Indicators

Malware leaves distinct patterns based on its purpose.

**Ransomware**

- **Primary Indicator:** Resource inaccessibility. User files become encrypted and inaccessible, with ransom notes (.README.txt, #DECRYPT_MY_FILES#.html) appearing on the desktop or in folders.
- **Secondary Indicators:** Outbound calls to command-and-control (C2) servers, unusual file extension changes (.locked, .crypt, .encrypted), and high CPU/disk activity during the encryption process.

### Trojan & Spyware/Keylogger

- **Trojan Indicator:** A seemingly legitimate program performing malicious actions in the background (e.g., unusual network connections from a "game").
- **Spyware/Keylogger Indicator:** Out-of-cycle logging or data exfiltration. Small, steady outbound data transfers to unknown IPs, capturing keystrokes, screenshots, or microphone data.

### Worm

- **Primary Indicator:** Rapid, horizontal spread and resource consumption. A single infected machine scans the network (high outbound connection attempts on common ports like 445/SMB, 22/SSH), infecting others, leading to a cascading network slowdown.

### Virus

- **Indicator:** Malicious code attached to legitimate executables. Signs include legitimate application files changing size or checksum, or antivirus alerts on common system files.

### Logic Bomb

- **Indicator:** Malicious activity triggered by a specific event or time. E.g., system crashes, or files are deleted every Friday the 13th, or after a specific employee is removed from the payroll system.

### Rootkit

- **Primary Indicator:** Missing logs and system subversion. The rootkit hides itself and other malware. Tools like ps, netstat, and ls show incorrect information. Antivirus fails to run or detect issues. The system feels "off" but direct inspection reveals nothing.

### Bloatware

- **Indicator:** Not typically malicious, but a performance indicator. Pre-installed, unwanted software consuming CPU, memory, and network bandwidth, often making the system a target for further exploitation due to poor performance and unpatched software.

## Section 2: The Physical World – Physical Attack Indicators

### Brute Force (Physical)

- **Indicator:** Damaged hardware. Signs of forced entry on doors, locks, or server racks. Broken keypads, damaged card readers.

**RFID Cloning**

- **Indicator:** Impossible travel or concurrent session usage. An employee's access badge is used to enter a building in New York at 9:00 AM and then in London at 9:15 AM. Logs show the same credentials used in two physically impossible locations nearly simultaneously.

**Environmental Attacks**

- **Indicator:** Unexpected system failure. HVAC failure leading to server room overheating (temperature sensors trigger alarms). Water damage, fire, or power anomalies causing widespread, correlated hardware failure.

## Section 3: The Traffic Flood – Network Attack Indicators

**Distributed Denial-of-Service (DDoS)**

- **Primary Indicator:** Resource inaccessibility for legitimate users due to massive, sustained inbound traffic from thousands of sources.
- **Amplified/Reflected DDoS:** Traffic volume is amplified (e.g., using DNS or NTP servers to send large responses to a small request) and appears to come from legitimate, reflected third-party servers. Logs show huge volumes of traffic from many IPs, all targeting a single service.

**DNS Attacks (Poisoning, DDoS)**

- **Indicator:** Blocked content or redirected traffic. Users are unable to reach legitimate websites (getting wrong IP addresses) or are redirected to malicious sites. DNS server logs show abnormal query loads or unauthorized zone transfer attempts.

**On-path Attack (Man-in-the-Middle)**

- **Indicator:** Unexpected certificate warnings in user browsers ("This connection is not private"), or detection of ARP table poisoning on the network. May also enable credential replay, where stolen session tokens are used from a different IP.

**Credential Replay**

- **Indicator:** Successful login from a new IP address using a valid session token or password shortly after a legitimate login, often without the user's typical behavioral pattern.

**Wireless Attacks**

- **Indicators:** Presence of rogue access points, users complaining about being disconnected and reconnected (deauth attacks), or unusual clients connected to the corporate Wi-Fi.

## Section 4: Exploiting the Code – Application Attack Indicators

### Injection (SQLi, Command Injection)

- **Indicator: Published/documented** error messages in web logs showing database syntax errors (e.g., "You have an error in your SQL syntax..."), or unexpected OS commands being executed.

### Buffer Overflow

- **Indicator:** Application or service crashes unexpectedly (resource inaccessibility), often with a memory access violation error. Followed by suspicious outbound connections from the crashed service.

### Privilege Escalation

- **Indicator:** A standard user account is suddenly performing actions or accessing files that require admin rights. Logs show a user account (jdoe) successfully using sudo or RUNAS commands they are not authorized for.

### Directory Traversal

- **Indicator:** Web server logs show HTTP requests containing patterns like ../../../../etc/passwd or ..\..\..\boot.ini attempting to access files outside of the web root.

### Replay Attack (Application Layer)

- **Indicator:** Identical, legitimate-looking requests (like a fund transfer) being submitted multiple times in quick succession.

### Forgery (CSRF, Clickjacking)

- **Indicator:** Users report actions they didn't perform (e.g., "I didn't change my email password") from their own authenticated sessions. Server logs show the action came from the user's valid IP and session.

## Section 5: Breaking the Math – Cryptographic & Password Attacks

### Cryptographic Attacks

- **Downgrade Attack: Indicated by** a secure connection (TLS 1.3) suddenly renegotiating to a weak protocol (SSL 2.0). Network tools show the connection using deprecated ciphers.
- **Collision/Birthday Attack:** Successful against weak hashes (MD5, SHA-1). Indicator: An indicator is when two different files or certificates producing the same hash value, undermining trust in digital signatures.

**Password Attacks**

- **Password Spraying:** Indicator: A single password (like "Spring2024!") failing across many different user accounts, triggering a few account lockouts but not mass lockouts. Logs show "Failed logon" for user1, user2, user3 with the same bad password.
- **Brute Force:** Indicator: Rapid, sequential login attempts against a single account, leading to a rapid account lockout. Logs show hundreds of "Failed logon" events for admin in seconds.

## Section 6: The Universal Clues – General Indicators

**General Indicators**

These are the high-level signs that *something* is wrong, regardless of the specific attack.

- **Account Lockout:** A user's account is repeatedly locked. Could indicate a brute-force attack, password spraying, or a compromised account being used elsewhere.
- **Concurrent Session Usage:** The same user account is logged in from two geographically distant locations at the same time. Indicates credential theft.
- **Blocked Content:** Security tools (proxies, IPS) are blocking traffic to known malicious sites or patterns. A sign that an infection is trying to "phone home."
- **Impossible Travel:** A user account shows logins from two cities thousands of miles apart within an hour. A near-certain sign of compromised credentials.
- **Resource Consumption:** CPU, memory, disk I/O, or network bandwidth is maxed out without a business reason. Indicates crypto-mining, DDoS participation, or a worm spreading.
- **Resource Inaccessibility:** Legitimate users cannot access a server, service, or their own files. Hallmark of DDoS, ransomware, or a system crash from an exploit.
- **Out-of-Cycle Logging & Missing Logs:** Logs are being generated at strange times (3 AM for an office workstation) or critical logs (firewall, authentication) have unexplained gaps. Indicates an attacker covering their tracks or a rootkit in action.
- **Published/Documented:** Security researchers or vendors publish advisories about a new vulnerability (CVE) being actively exploited in the wild. This is an external indicator that you should check your systems.

## Chapter Summary

Being a security analyst is like being a doctor for your network. You look at the symptoms (indicators) to diagnose the disease (attack).

- **Performance Issues (Resource Consumption/Inaccessibility):** Think DDoS, worms, ransomware, crypto-mining.
- **Log Anomalies (Lockouts, Impossible Travel, Missing Logs):** Think credential theft, brute force, rootkits.
- **User Reports (Can't access files, weird pop-ups):** Think ransomware, spyware, phishing.
- **Network Alerts (Blocked content, strange traffic patterns):** Think malware C2, on-path attacks, injection attempts.

The key is correlation. A single failed login is noise. 100 failed logins in a minute for one account is a brute-force attack. That account then successfully logging in from a new country is a confirmed compromise.

**Exam-Related Tips**

1. Ransomware = Can't access files + ransom note. This is almost always the right answer if those two clues are present.
2. Impossible Travel = Stolen credentials. No other explanation.
3. Account Lockout: Distinguish Brute Force (many attempts on *one* account) from Password Spraying (one attempt on *many* accounts).
4. Resource Consumption + Network Spread = Worm.
5. Missing Logs + System "Feels Hacked" but Scans Clean = Rootkit.

**Think Like the Exam**

*Scenario: "A security analyst reviews SIEM alerts. One alert shows the corporate web server's CPU sustained at 98% for an hour. Another alert shows the same server is generating massive outbound traffic to hundreds of external IPs on port 22. User reports indicate the company website is extremely slow. What type of attack is MOST likely occurring?"*

- **Clue 1:** High CPU (Resource Consumption).
- **Clue 2:** Massive outbound SSH (port 22) traffic to many IPs. This is scanning/propagation behavior.

- **Clue 3:** Website is slow (Resource Inaccessibility for users).
- **Conclusion:** The server is compromised and is actively trying to spread to other systems via SSH. This is the classic behavior of a *Worm*.

**Self-Reflection Prompt**

Check your own email spam folder. Find one phishing email. Now, play detective: What are the indicators in that email that signaled to the spam filter that it was malicious? (e.g., suspicious sender address, malicious links, urgency language). This trains you to spot the breadcrumbs left by attackers in their very first contact attempt.

# Chapter 9 – Building Your Digital Fort: Enterprise Mitigation Techniques

## Exam Objective 2.5:
## Explain the purpose of mitigation techniques used to secure the enterprise

*Chapter Introduction*

You can identify the attackers, the vulnerabilities, and the signs of an attack. Now, what do you actually *do* about it? This chapter is all about defense—the proactive and reactive measures you build into an organization to reduce risk, limit damage, and kick out intruders. We're moving from theory to action. These aren't just fancy terms; they're the blueprint for building a resilient security program. From the broad strategy of network segmentation to the specific action of changing a default password, every technique here serves a clear purpose in the CIA Triad and the principle of *defense in depth*. For the Security+ exam, you need to know not just *what* each technique is, but *why* you use it and *what problem* it solves.

**Security+ Exam Mindset**

For this objective, CompTIA tests purpose and application. You'll get scenarios like: "To prevent a compromised point-of-sale system from accessing the corporate database, what should be implemented?" You must select the correct mitigation (e.g., Segmentation). Focus on understanding the *security goal* of each control: Does it prevent, detect, contain, or recover?

## Section 1: The Big Picture Strategies

These techniques shape the entire security architecture.

**Segmentation**

- **What it is:** Dividing a network into smaller, isolated zones or segments (e.g., separating the finance department network from the guest Wi-Fi).
- **Purpose:** Containment. It limits an attacker's ability to move laterally ("east-west") across the network. If the marketing department gets infected with malware, segmentation prevents it from easily spreading to the R&D servers.

- **Real-World Example:** A retail company puts all its point-of-sale (POS) systems on a dedicated network segment that cannot initiate connections to the internet, only to a specific payment processor. This dramatically reduces the attack surface for credit card theft.

**Isolation**

- **What it is:** Taking segmentation to the extreme. It's the complete separation of a system or network from others.
- **Purpose:** Maximum containment for high-risk assets. Used for air-gapped networks (physically isolated), quarantined malware analysis labs, or sensitive R&D environments.
- **Key Difference from Segmentation:** Segmentation allows controlled communication between zones. Isolation aims to allow *none*.

**Least Privilege**

- **What it is:** The principle of granting users and systems only the minimum levels of access (permissions) absolutely necessary to perform their job functions.
- **Purpose:** Reduces the impact of compromise. If a user's account is hacked, the attacker only gets that user's limited privileges, not administrator access to the entire domain.
- **Real-World Analogy:** A bank teller has a key to the cash drawer (their job) but not to the main vault (the administrator's job).

## Section 2: Controlling Access

These techniques define who and what can interact with your resources.

**Access Control & Permissions**

- **Access Control List (ACL):** A list of rules applied to a resource (file, folder, network share) that specifies which users or system processes are granted access.
- **Permissions:** The specific rights (Read, Write, Execute, Modify) granted within an ACL.
- **Purpose:** Enforces confidentiality and integrity. They are the technical implementation of the least privilege principle, directly controlling who can see or change data.

**Application Allow List**

- **What it is:** (Formerly Whitelisting). A security policy that allows *only* pre-approved software to run on a system. All other software is blocked by default.

- **Purpose:** Prevents malware execution and unauthorized software. It's a powerful preventive control, especially on static systems like servers or kiosks. It stops zero-day malware that hasn't been seen before because the malware isn't on the approved list.
- **Contrast with Deny List (Blacklist):** A deny list blocks known-bad software. An allow list is more secure because the default is DENY.

## Section 3: The Maintenance Cycle

Security is not a one-time setup; it's continuous maintenance.

### Patching

- **What it is:** Applying updates (patches) from vendors to fix security vulnerabilities and bugs in operating systems and applications.
- **Purpose:** Remediates known vulnerabilities. It is the single most effective mitigation against the vast majority of attacks that exploit published flaws. Patching closes the doors that attackers are trying to walk through.

### Configuration Enforcement

- **What it is:** Using tools and policies to ensure all systems are configured according to secure baselines (e.g., disabling unnecessary services, setting correct file permissions).
- **Purpose:** Fights misconfiguration, the #1 cause of breaches. Automated tools scan systems and automatically remediate any configuration "drift" back to the secure standard.

### Decommissioning

- **What it is:** The secure, formal process of retiring old hardware, software, or services.
- **Purpose:** Eliminates forgotten attack surfaces. An old, forgotten server running Windows 2003 is a ticking time bomb. Proper decommissioning includes data sanitization (wiping drives), asset tracking updates, and physical destruction.

## Section 4: The Core Protections

Foundational techniques that protect data at rest and in transit.

### Encryption

- **Purpose:** Protects the *confidentiality* of data. Renders data unreadable without the proper key, mitigating the impact of theft (a stolen laptop with Full-Disk Encryption) or interception (TLS for web traffic).

**Monitoring**

- **What it is:** The continuous collection and analysis of data from logs, network traffic (IDS/IPS), and endpoints (EDR).
- **Purpose:** Enables detection and response. You cannot stop what you cannot see. Monitoring provides the visibility needed to identify indicators of malicious activity (from Objective 2.4) and trigger incident response.

## Section 5: Host Hardening Techniques

These are the specific actions you take on individual computers and servers to make them more resistant to attack.

**Installation of Endpoint Protection**

- **Purpose:** Prevents, detects, and removes malware. This is the antivirus/anti-malware/EDR (Endpoint Detection and Response) software running on every laptop, desktop, and server.

**Host-Based Firewall**

- **Purpose:** Filters network traffic to and from the single host. It provides a local layer of segmentation, blocking unauthorized connections even if the network firewall is misconfigured.

**Host-Based Intrusion Prevention System (HIPS)**

- **Purpose:** Monitors and analyzes system activity on the host for malicious behavior (e.g., unauthorized registry changes, suspicious process injection) and can block it in real-time.

**Disabling Unused Ports & Protocols**

- **Purpose:** Reduces attack surface. If a service isn't running (e.g., Telnet on port 23, SMBv1), it cannot be exploited. This is a fundamental hardening step.

**Changing Default Passwords**

- **Purpose:** Prevents trivial credential-based attacks. Default passwords are public knowledge. Changing them is the bare minimum of security hygiene for any device (routers, IoT cameras, network switches).

**Removal of Unnecessary Software**

- **Purpose:** Reduces attack surface and bloat. Fewer applications mean fewer applications to patch and fewer potential vulnerabilities. This includes removing bloatware from new PCs and old, unused programs from servers.

# Chapter Summary

Mitigation techniques are your security building blocks. You use them in layers:

1. **Design & Architecture:** Start with Segmentation, Isolation, and Least Privilege to create a secure foundation.
2. **Access & Execution Control:** Implement Access Control Lists, Permissions, and Application Allow Lists to define precisely what can be accessed and run.
3. **System Hardening: Harden** each host by disabling ports, changing defaults, removing software, and installing endpoint protection, HIPS, and host firewalls.
4. **Ongoing Maintenance:** Sustain security through Patching, Configuration Enforcement, and Monitoring.
5. **Data Protection:** Apply Encryption to protect data itself.
6. **Lifecycle End:** Securely Decommission assets that are no longer needed.

The overarching principle is Defense in Depth (DiD)—no single mitigation is perfect, so you use many overlapping controls. If one fails (the firewall is bypassed), another (host-based IPS) might catch the attack.

**Exam-Related Tips**

1. Segmentation is the answer to questions about containing breaches or protecting sensitive network zones.
2. Least Privilege is the answer to limiting damage from insider threats or compromised user accounts.
3. Application Allow List is stronger than antivirus (deny list) for preventing unknown malware.
4. Patching is the direct mitigation for exploits against known vulnerabilities.
5. Hardening is a group of specific actions; know the purpose of each common one (disable ports, change defaults, etc.).

**Think Like the Exam**

*Scenario: "A systems administrator is preparing a new web server for production. The server will host a public-facing application. Which of the following hardening techniques would be MOST effective in preventing the server from being used as a relay for attacks on other internal systems?"*

- The goal is to prevent the server from attacking *other internal systems*.
- A public-facing server needs to talk to the internet, but perhaps not to the internal finance server.
- Installing a Host-Based Firewall would allow the administrator to create granular rules. They could allow necessary inbound/outbound web traffic but block all outbound connections from the web server to internal IP ranges. This is a form of local segmentation and containment.

**Self-Reflection Prompt**

Look at your own computer (or phone). Pick three hardening techniques from this list. Have you, or could you, apply them to your device? (e.g., Do you have a host firewall enabled? Are all unnecessary apps/ports disabled? Is your software auto-patching?) This connects enterprise security to personal security, which is where good security habits start.

# Domain 3:
# Security Architecture

# Chapter 10 – The Shape of Security: Comparing Architecture Models

## Exam Objective 3.1:

## Compare and contrast security implications of different architecture models.

*Chapter Introduction*

Think of security architecture as the blueprint for your digital city. You can build a sprawling, open-plan metropolis (a flat network), a fortified castle with a moat (on-premises data center), or a dynamic, floating city in the clouds (public cloud). Each design has dramatically different security implications, strengths, and weaknesses. This chapter is your guided tour through the major architectural models powering today's world—from the familiar cloud to the specialized systems controlling power grids. For the Security+ exam, you need to think like a security architect: given a business need, which model offers the right balance of security, cost, and flexibility? You'll be comparing and contrasting these models constantly.

**Security+ Exam Mindset**

This objective is all about trade-offs and security ownership. CompTIA will present scenarios that force you to choose the most appropriate architecture based on security requirements like data sovereignty, availability, or the need to patch quickly. You must understand the shared responsibility model of the cloud intimately, and be able to contrast the control of on-premises with the scalability of cloud or the agility of containers.

## Section 1: The Cloud Revolution & Its Shared Responsibility

**Cloud Models & The Responsibility Matrix**

The core security implication of the cloud is the Shared Responsibility Model. Security is a joint effort between the Cloud Service Provider (CSP) and *you*, the customer.

- **IaaS (Infrastructure as a Service):** CSP secures the cloud infrastructure (physical data centers, network, hypervisors). *You* secure everything you put on it: OS, apps, data, firewalls.

- **PaaS (Platform as a Service):** CSP secures infrastructure and the platform (OS, runtime). *You* secure your applications and data.
- **SaaS (Software as a Service):** CSP secures almost everything (infrastructure, platform, application). *You* are primarily responsible for securing your data, access controls, and user behavior.

**The Exam Clue:** If a question is about a vulnerability in the underlying hypervisor, that's the CSP's problem in IaaS/PaaS/SaaS. If it's about a misconfigured S3 bucket, that's *your* problem, even in the cloud.

**Hybrid & Third-Party Considerations**

- **Hybrid Cloud:** Mix of on-prem and cloud. *Security Implication:* Complexity! You now have *two* security perimeters to manage, and data moving between them. Consistent identity management and encryption in transit are critical.
- **Third-Party Vendors:** Using cloud services means relying on the CSP's security. You must perform due diligence (review their audits, SOC 2 reports) because their risk becomes your risk.

## Section 2: The Modern Infrastructure Toolkit

**Infrastructure as Code (IaC)**

- **What it is:** Managing and provisioning infrastructure through machine-readable definition files (code) rather than manual processes.
- **Security Implication:** Consistency and reduced human error. IaC templates ensure every deployment is identical and follows the secure baseline. However, a vulnerability in the IaC template will be propagated to every system it deploys. Version control for IaC is a security requirement.

**Serverless & Microservices**

- **Serverless (e.g., AWS Lambda):** You write code; the CSP manages the servers. *Security Implication:* You lose visibility into the OS/network layer. Security focuses on securing the function code, managing dependencies for vulnerabilities, and strict access permissions for the function's execution role.
- **Microservices:** An application is built as a suite of small, independent services. *Security Implication:* Increased attack surface. Each service has its own API that must be secured. Requires robust service authentication (like service meshes) and API security.

**Containerization (e.g., Docker)**

- **What it is:** Packaging an application with all its dependencies into a lightweight, portable "container."
- **Security vs. Virtualization:** Containers share the host OS kernel, unlike VMs, which have separate kernels. *Implication:* A kernel exploit can break container isolation (a more severe form of "escape"). Security requires securing the container image (scanning for vulns), the host OS, and using minimal, trusted base images.

**Virtualization**

- **What it is:** Running multiple virtual machines (VMs) with separate OSes on a single physical host.
- **Primary Security Concern:** VM Escape (breaking out of the guest VM to the host hypervisor). This requires keeping the hypervisor patched and hardened.

## Section 3: Network & Physical Architecture

**Physical Isolation & Air-Gapping**

- **Air-Gapped:** A network physically isolated from other networks (no wireless, no physical cables). *Security Implication:* Ultimate security against remote attacks, but impractical for most uses, and data transfer requires physical media (USB), which becomes a major risk vector.

**Logical Segmentation & SDN**

- **Logical Segmentation (VLANs):** Using software to create separate network segments on the same physical hardware. *Purpose:* To contain breaches, improve performance, and facilitate management.
- **Software-Defined Networking (SDN):** Separates the network control plane (the brain) from the data plane (the muscle). *Security Implication:* Enables dynamic, granular security policies (microsegmentation) but centralizes risk, compromising the SDN controller, which can compromise the entire network.

### On-Premises vs. Cloud

| Consideration | On-Premises | Cloud |
|---|---|---|
| **Control** | Full control over hardware, network, and data physical location. | Less control. Reliant on CSP for physical/infrastructure security. |
| **Cost** | High capital expenditure (CapEx) for hardware. | Operational expenditure (OpEx), pay-as-you-go. |
| **Scalability** | Slow and difficult. Requires purchasing/installing new hardware. | Instant and elastic. Scale up/down with clicks/API calls. |
| **Security Responsibility** | You are responsible for everything, from the door lock to the database. | Shared responsibility. You manage your data, identity, and configurations. |

### Centralized vs. Decentralized

- **Centralized (e.g., Active Directory):** One central point of control for policies and authentication. *Security Implication:* Efficient management, but a single point of failure. A compromise of the central system (like a domain controller) is catastrophic.
- **Decentralized (e.g., Peer-to-Peer):** No central authority. *Security Implication:* More resilient to single-point failure, but much harder to enforce consistent security policies and detect anomalies.

## Section 4: Specialized Systems

### IoT and Embedded Systems

- **Characteristics:** Limited compute, memory, and power; often headless, meaning they have no interface. Security Implications: Inability to patch, weak default passwords, and long device lifespans. They become permanent, vulnerable entry points to networks.

### ICS/SCADA

- **What it is:** Systems that control industrial processes (power grids, water treatment, manufacturing).

- **Security Implications:** Availability is paramount. Patching is difficult due to 24/7 uptime requirements. Often use proprietary, legacy protocols with no security features. A breach can have physical world consequences (destroy equipment, cut power).

**Real-Time Operating System (RTOS)**

- **What it is:** An OS designed for deterministic, predictable timing (e.g., in cars, medical devices).
- **Security Implication:** Security is often retrofitted as an afterthought. Traditional security scans can interfere with real-time guarantees. Vulnerabilities can be life-threatening.

**Section 5: The Architect's Checklist – Key Considerations**

**Key Considerations**

When comparing models, always weigh these factors:

- **Availability & High Availability (HA):** How resistant is the architecture to downtime? HA designs use redundancy (multiple servers, data centers) to ensure uptime.
- **Resilience:** The ability to recover from failures and continue operating.
- **Cost: CapEx vs. OpEx.** Cloud transfers hardware costs to operational fees.
- **Scalability & Responsiveness:** Can the architecture handle sudden growth (scalability) and deliver performance (responsiveness)?
- **Ease of Deployment & Recovery:** How quickly can you deploy new services (IaC, cloud) or restore from a disaster (backups, snapshots)?
- **Risk Transference:** The use of cloud or a third-party transfers some risk (physical theft, power failure) but introduces new risks (misconfiguration, provider outage).
- **Patch Availability & Inability to Patch:** Standard systems get patches; many IoT, ICS, and embedded systems do not, creating permanent risk.
- **Power & Compute:** Physical constraints. A remote IoT sensor has a limited battery and CPU, preventing it from running strong encryption or host-based IPS.

# Chapter Summary

Choosing an architecture is a series of security trade-offs. The cloud offers scalability and transfers physical risk, but requires you to master the shared responsibility model and secure your configurations. On-premises gives you full control but requires you to bear all costs and expertise. Modern paradigms like containers, serverless, and microservices offer agility but introduce new attack surfaces (APIs, shared kernels). Specialized systems (IoT, ICS) prioritize availability and function over security, making them uniquely vulnerable. As a security professional, your role is to understand these implications and guide the business toward the architecture that best aligns security with organizational goals.

**Exam-Related Tips**

1. **Shared Responsibility is the Primary Consideration:** Be ready to identify who is responsible (customer vs. CSP) in any cloud scenario.
2. **Containers share the OS kernel; VMs do not.** This is a key differentiator.
3. **IoT/ICS = Availability > Confidentiality/Integrity.** Patching is often impossible.
4. **Hybrid = Increased Complexity.** Think about secure data transfer and unified identity.
5. **IaC:** Security is in the template. A bad template creates many insecure systems.

**Think Like the Exam**

*Scenario: "A development team wants to rapidly deploy a new, event-driven application that will experience unpredictable, spiky traffic. The team wants to focus solely on writing application code without managing servers. Which architecture model best meets these requirements, and what is a primary security concern for this model?"*

- Requirements: Rapid deploy, spiky traffic, no server management.
- This is the perfect use case for *Serverless* computing (like AWS Lambda).
- The primary security concern shifts to securing the application code and its dependencies and strictly defining the execution role permissions (least privilege) to prevent the function from accessing unauthorized resources.

**Self-Reflection Prompt**

Consider a modern smart home (IoT lights, thermostat, voice assistant) versus a traditional industrial factory (ICS/SCADA). Both have "connected devices," but their *architecture considerations* are worlds apart. List 2-3 security trade-offs each one makes. (e.g., The smart home prioritizes ease of use and cost over security; the factory prioritizes 24/7 availability over patching). This reinforces the concept that architecture is driven by purpose.

# Chapter 11 – Building the Defenses: Applying Security to Infrastructure

## Exam Objective 3.2:

## Given a scenario, apply security principles to secure enterprise infrastructure

*Chapter Introduction*

You've chosen your architectural model (cloud, hybrid, on-premises). Now it's time to build the actual defenses within it. This chapter is the *hands-on, tactical guide* to placing and configuring the security devices and controls that protect your network. Think of it as setting up security checkpoints, surveillance cameras, and secure tunnels in your digital city. Where do you put the firewall? How do you secure a switch port? Should your IPS fail-open or fail-closed during a power outage? For the Security+ exam, you'll be given a detailed infrastructure scenario and must select the correct security controls and configurations to meet specific security goals.

**Security+ Exam Mindset**

This is a *practical, scenario-heavy* objective. CompTIA will describe a network layout, a business requirement (e.g., "secure remote access for sales staff"), or a security problem (e.g., "prevent SQL injection on the web server"). You must choose the right technology (e.g., WAF, VPN) and understand its proper implementation (e.g., device placement, failover mode). Focus on the "why" behind each placement and setting.

## Section 1: Strategic Placement & Design

How and where you place a security device is as important as having it.

**Device Placement & Security Zones**

- **Device Placement:** A firewall placed *inside* the network protects specific segments; one placed at the perimeter protects everything inside from the outside.
- **Security Zones:** Logical segments with different trust levels. A common model:
    1. **Untrusted Zone:** The public Internet.
    2. **Demilitarized Zone (DMZ):** Semi-trusted. Houses public-facing servers (web, email). Access from outside is allowed *only* to the DMZ.

3. **Trusted Zone (Internal Network):** Contains internal workstations and servers. Traffic from the DMZ to the Internal zone is tightly restricted.

**Principle Applied**

This follows segmentation and defense in depth. An attacker breaching the web server in the DMZ still faces another firewall to reach the internal database.

**Attack Surface & Connectivity**

- **Attack Surface:** The sum of all points where an attacker can try to enter or extract data. **Principle:** Minimize it.
- **Connectivity:** Who can talk to whom? The principle of least privilege applies to networks: a user's PC doesn't need direct connectivity to the domain controller; it can go through approved paths.

**Real-World Example:** An IoT thermostat on the corporate network should be placed on a dedicated IoT zone that only has connectivity to its cloud service, not to internal file shares. This reduces its attack surface.

**Failure Modes: Fail-Open vs. Fail-Closed**

- **Fail-Open:** If the security device fails, it allows all traffic to pass. Used when availability is more important than security (e.g., a front door to a hospital in a fire).
- **Fail-Closed:** If the security device fails, it blocks all traffic. Used when security is more important than availability (e.g., a firewall protecting a nuclear plant's control network).

**Exam Clue:** A scenario discussing a "security gate" at a data center that locks during a power outage is describing a fail-closed physical control. For network devices, a fail-closed firewall is generally safer.

## Section 2: Choosing & Positioning Network Appliances

**Device Attributes**

- **Active vs. Passive:**
    - **Active (Inline):** Devices that sit in the traffic path and can block traffic (e.g., firewall, IPS). They can cause a single point of failure.
    - **Passive (Tap/SPAN):** Devices that copy traffic for analysis but don't block it (e.g., IDS, monitoring sensor). They don't impact network performance or availability if they fail.

- **Inline vs. Tap/Monitor:** This is the physical/logical implementation of active vs. passive.

**Key Network Appliances & Their Security Role**

- **Jump Server (Bastion Host):** A heavily fortified server that provides the **only** point of entry (a single "jump") into a secure zone (like a production network). All admin access must go through it for auditing and control.
- **Proxy Server:** An intermediary for user requests. A forward proxy hides internal clients from the Internet. A reverse proxy protects servers from direct client access, can perform SSL offloading, and acts as a WAF.
- **IPS vs. IDS**
    - **Intrusion Prevention System (IPS): Active/Inline.** Analyzes traffic and can block malicious packets in real-time.
    - **Intrusion Detection System (IDS): Passive/Tap.** Analyzes copied traffic and alerts on malicious activity.
- **Load Balancer:** Distributes traffic across multiple servers. **Security Role:** Hides individual servers, can filter traffic, and provides a single point to enforce TLS/SSL policies.
- **Sensors:** Devices (like a network tap or a dedicated IDS appliance) placed strategically to monitor traffic in key segments (e.g., before and after the firewall, in the DMZ).

**Port Security (802.1X & EAP)**

- **What it is:** A standard for Network Access Control (NAC). It prevents unauthorized devices from connecting to a wired or wireless network.
- **How it works:** When a device connects to a switch port, the switch (authenticator) uses a RADIUS server (authentication server) and the Extensible Authentication Protocol (EAP) to authenticate the device/user (supplicant) before granting network access.
- **Principle Applied: Implicit deny.** The port is "closed" until authentication succeeds. This stops rogue devices.

## Section 3: The Firewall Family

Different firewalls solve different security problems.

- **Layer 4 Firewall (Stateful):** Makes decisions based on IP addresses, ports, and connection state. "Does this packet belong to an established TCP session?"

- **Layer 7 Firewall Next-Generation Firewall (NGFW):** Adds application awareness and user identity. Can block specific apps (Facebook, BitTorrent) and enforce policies based on user, not just IP.
- **Web Application Firewall (WAF):** Specialized for protecting web applications. Analyzes HTTP/HTTPS traffic for SQLi, XSS, and other OWASP Top 10 attacks. Placed in front of web servers.
- **Unified Threat Management (UTM):** An "all-in-one" box combining firewall, IPS, antivirus, content filtering, etc. Good for small businesses; can be a single point of failure.

## Section 4: Secure Access & Communication

### Virtual Private Network (VPN) & Remote Access

- **Purpose:** Creates a secure, encrypted tunnel over an untrusted network (the Internet).
- **Site-to-Site VPN:** Connects two entire networks (e.g., office to cloud VPC).
- **Remote Access VPN:** Connects individual users to a network. Critical for secure work-from-home.

### Tunneling Protocols

- **Transport Layer Security (TLS):** Used for modern remote access VPNs (often in a browser) and securing web traffic (HTTPS). Operates at a higher layer.
- **Internet Protocol Security (IPsec):** A suite of protocols that operates at the network layer (Layer 3). Commonly used for site-to-site VPNs. Provides confidentiality, integrity, and authentication.

### SD-WAN & SASE (The Modern Edge)

- **Software-Defined WAN (SD-WAN):** Intelligently routes traffic between branch offices and data centers over multiple connections (MPLS, broadband, 5G). **Security Implication:** Can reduce cost, but you must still secure each connection.
- **Secure Access Service Edge (SASE):** The convergence of network security (FWaaS, CASB, SWG) and WAN capabilities (SD-WAN) into a single, cloud-delivered service. **Principle:** Security follows the user/device, not the network location. Ideal for a mobile, cloud-first workforce.

## Section 5: The Art of Selection – Effective Controls

### Effective Controls

Given a scenario, you must select controls that are:

1. **Appropriate:** A WAF won't protect against a phishing email. An IPS won't stop an insider copying files to a USB.
2. **Cost-Effective:** Don't deploy a $100k appliance for a 10-person office. A UTM might be perfect.
3. **Layered (Defense in Depth):** Don't rely on just a firewall. Add IPS, endpoint protection, and user training.
4. **Operationally Sustainable:** Can your team manage it? A fail-closed, complex IPS that nobody understands will either be misconfigured or disabled, making it useless.

# Chapter Summary

Securing infrastructure is a puzzle of placement, configuration, and selection. You place devices to create security zones and control traffic flow. You configure them with the right failure mode for their mission. You select specialized appliances (WAF, Proxy, Load Balancer) to protect specific assets. You implement port security (802.1X) to keep rogue devices off your network. And you provide secure access through VPNs, SD-WAN, and SASE models. Every decision should be guided by core principles: minimize attack surface, segment, enforce least privilege, and plan for failure.

**Exam-Related Tips**

1. **IPS = Inline (Block), IDS = Passive (Alert).** This is a must-know distinction.
2. **WAF = Protects Web Apps** from SQLi/XSS. It's not a general firewall.
3. **802.1X = "Port-based NAC."** The answer for "preventing unauthorized devices on the network."
4. **Fail-Open vs. Fail-Closed:** Relate it to the priority in the scenario: **Safety/Availability (Open)** vs. **Security/Safety (Closed)**.
5. **Jump Server = Admin Access Control.** The answer for "how to securely manage servers in a secure zone."

**Think Like the Exam**

*Scenario: "A company's public website was defaced by a SQL injection attack. The web server is hosted in an on-premises DMZ. Which of the following controls, placed in the correct location, would be MOST effective in preventing a recurrence of this specific attack type?"*

- **The Attack:** SQL Injection.
- **The Target:** A public web server in the DMZ.
- **Needed Control:** Something that inspects HTTP/HTTPS traffic for malicious SQL patterns.
- **Correct Answer:** Implement a Web Application Firewall (WAF) and place it in front of the web server (between the Internet and the server, ideally in the DMZ). A traditional firewall (Layer 4) or an IPS might not have the deep application-layer inspection needed to catch SQLi.

**Self-Reflection Prompt**

Draw a simple diagram of a home network (Router, your laptop, a smart TV). Now, sketch where you would place security "zones" and controls if this were a micro-enterprise. Where would you put a firewall? What devices would go in an "IoT Zone"? How would you enable secure "remote access" to your laptop? This visual exercise cements the concepts of placement and zoning.

# Chapter 12 – The Crown Jewels: Strategies to Protect Data

## Exam Objective 3.3: Compare and contrast concepts and strategies to protect data

*Chapter Introduction*

Data is the lifeblood of the modern enterprise and the ultimate target for attackers. This chapter answers the most critical questions in security: *What data do you have?* (Classification), *Where is it?* (State and Sovereignty), and most importantly, *How do you protect it?* (Methods). We'll move from high-level concepts like "trade secret" and "data sovereignty" to the hands-on tactics of tokenization and encryption. For the Security+ exam, you must understand that not all data is created equal, and you don't protect a public marketing brochure the same way you protect customer credit card numbers. Your defense strategy must be as nuanced as the data itself.

**Security+ Exam Mindset**

This objective tests your ability to classify, prioritize, and select appropriate controls for data protection. Expect questions that ask: "What classification should this document have?" or "Which method is best for protecting credit card data in a database?" You'll need to match data types to classifications, and classifications to the proper security methods. Think in layers: first identify, then classify, then protect based on state and location.

## Section 1: What Are We Protecting? – Data Types

**Data Types**

Understanding the *nature* of data dictates its sensitivity and the legal rules around it.

- **Regulated Data:** Data protected by law or industry standards. **Examples:** Personal Health Information (PHI) under HIPAA, Payment Card Industry (PCI) data, and Personally Identifiable Information (PII) under GDPR. **Implication:** Mishandling it results in fines and legal penalties.
- **Trade Secret & Intellectual Property (IP):** The "secret sauce" that gives a business its competitive edge. **Examples:** The Coca-Cola formula, proprietary algorithms, unreleased product designs. **Implication:** Loss leads to loss of competitive advantage.

- **Legal & Financial Information:** Contracts, merger details, accounting records, bank statements. **Implication:** Loss leads to legal liability, fraud, and financial loss.
- **Human-Readable vs. Non-Human-Readable:**
    - **Human-Readable:** Data in a format people can understand (documents, emails, clear-text logs).
    - **Non-Human-Readable (Machine Data):** Database files, encrypted data, binary executables. Often requires tools or keys to interpret.

## Section 2: How Sensitive Is It? – Data Classifications

### Data Classifications

Classification is the process of labeling data based on its sensitivity and impact if disclosed or altered. It's the cornerstone of data protection.

| Classification | Definition & Examples | Typical Handling Requirements |
|---|---|---|
| **Public** | Data intended for public release. Press releases, marketing brochures. | Minimal protection. Integrity is key to prevent defacement. |
| **Private (or Internal Use)** | Internal data not for public release, but disclosure wouldn't cause severe harm. Internal memos, policies. | Basic access controls within the company. |
| **Confidential** | Sensitive data where unauthorized disclosure could cause moderate damage to the organization. Employee records, internal financial reports. | Strong access controls (need-to-know), encryption at rest and in transit. |
| **Sensitive / Restricted** | Highly sensitive data where unauthorized disclosure could cause severe damage. Regulated data (PHI, PCI), trade secrets. | Strictest controls: strong encryption, strict access logs, data loss prevention (DLP). |
| **Critical** | Data essential for business operations. Loss or corruption would cause immediate and catastrophic operational failure. Examples: Active Directory database, core transaction logs. | Focus on availability and integrity. Redundant, highly available systems with frequent backups. |

**Why Classification Matters:** It tells employees *how to handle* the data and tells IT *what security controls to apply.* You spend more resources protecting "Restricted" data than "Public" data.

## Section 3: The Where and When – General Data Considerations

**Data States: The Lifecycle of Data**

- **Data at Rest:** Stored on a medium (disk, SSD, USB, cloud storage). **Primary Risk:** Theft of the storage device/media. **Primary Mitigation:** Encryption (Full-Disk, File, Database).
- **Data in Transit:** Moving across a network (LAN, WAN, Internet). **Primary Risk:** Interception (eavesdropping, on-path attacks). Primary Mitigation: Encryption (TLS, IPsec, VPN).
- **Data in Use:** Being actively processed by a CPU in memory (RAM). **Primary Risk:** Memory scraping attacks, unauthorized access by other processes. **Primary Mitigation: Hardest to protect.** Use secure processing environments (secure enclaves), memory encryption.

**Data Sovereignty & Geolocation**

- **Data Sovereignty:** The concept that data is subject to the laws and governance of the country where it is physically located.
- **Geolocation:** The physical geographic location of data.
- **Why It Matters:** Regulations like GDPR may **require** that EU citizens' data stay within the EU. A U.S. company using a cloud provider must know if their data might be stored in a data center in a country with lax privacy laws. **Mitigation:** Use cloud provider tools to enforce geographic restrictions (e.g., only store data in the us-east-1 region).

## Section 4: The Toolbox – Methods to Secure Data

**Securing Data**

Now we apply specific controls based on classification, state, and location.

- **Geographic Restrictions:** A policy or technical control that prevents data from being stored or processed in unauthorized jurisdictions. Enforces **data sovereignty**.
- **Encryption:** The gold standard for protecting the confidentiality of data at rest and in transit. Renders data unreadable without the key. Use strong, modern algorithms (AES-256, TLS 1.3).

- **Hashing:** Protects integrity, not confidentiality. Used to verify files haven't been altered (checksums), and to securely store passwords (with a salt).
- **Data Masking & Tokenization (De-identification):**
  - **Masking:** Obscuring specific data within a dataset (e.g., showing XXX-XX-1234 for an SSN). Used in non-production environments (development, testing).
  - **Tokenization:** Replacing sensitive data with a non-sensitive equivalent (a token). The real data is stored in a secure token vault. The token is worthless if stolen. Ideal for payment processing systems (PCI DSS).
- **Obfuscation:** Making data difficult to understand (e.g., steganography, code obfuscation). Weak security – provides "security through obscurity," not real cryptographic protection.
- **Segmentation:** Isolating sensitive data onto its own secure network segment or database instance. Limits lateral movement; if the web server is compromised, the segmented database is not automatically exposed.
- **Permission Restrictions:** The implementation of least privilege at the data level. Using access control lists (ACLs) to ensure only authorized users/applications can read, write, or execute specific data.

# Chapter Summary

Data protection is a systematic process:

1. **Identify and Classify:** What data do you have? Is it Public, Confidential, or Restricted?
2. **Understand its Context:** Where is it? (At rest, in transit, in use) And under whose laws? (Sovereignty).
3. **Apply Tailored Controls:**
    - For Confidentiality: Use Encryption (for data at rest/in transit) and Tokenization (for specific datasets like payment cards).
    - For Integrity: Use Hashing.
    - For Access Control: Use Permission Restrictions and Segmentation.
    - For Regulatory Compliance: Use Geographic Restrictions and Masking for test data.

The most sensitive data (Restricted, Critical) gets the full suite of controls. The goal is to make data useless to an attacker even if they bypass some defenses.

**Exam-Related Tips**

1. Encryption for Confidentiality, Hashing for Integrity. Don't mix them up.
2. Tokenization vs. Masking: Tokenization is for production (uses a vault). Masking is for non-production (irreversible obfuscation).
3. Data Sovereignty = Legal Jurisdiction. The answer often involves geographic restrictions in cloud settings.
4. Classification Drives Controls. If a scenario mentions "trade secret" or "PHI," the data is Restricted or Sensitive, and the correct controls will be strong (encryption, strict ACLs).
5. Data in Use is the hardest to protect; it's often the weak link.

**Think Like the Exam**

*Scenario: "A company needs to process customer credit card transactions. To reduce PCI DSS compliance scope and minimize risk, they want to ensure the actual credit card numbers are never stored in their transactional database. Which data security method should it implement?"*

- **Goal:** Keep real credit card numbers out of the database to reduce risk and compliance scope.

- **Encryption** would store the numbers in the database (just in encrypted form), which still falls under PCI scope.
- **Masking** only obscures part of the number; the full number might still be present.
- **Tokenization** replaces the real number with a random token. The real number is sent to a secure, PCI-compliant vault managed by a third party. The database only stores the token. This is the correct answer as it achieves the goal.

**Self-Reflection Prompt**

Look at an email in your inbox. Try to classify it: Is it Public, Private, or Confidential? What data type is it (e.g., financial, personal)? Now, what protection methods is your email provider likely applying to it at rest and in transit? This connects everyday experience to enterprise data protection frameworks.

# Chapter 13 – When Things Go Wrong: Resilience & Recovery

## Exam Objective 3.4:

## Explain the importance of resilience and recovery in security architecture

*Chapter Introduction*

Here's the hard truth: breaches and disasters *will* happen. A sophisticated attacker, a freak storm, or a simple human error can bring your operations to a halt. Security architecture isn't just about building walls to keep threats out—it's about building a system that can absorb a hit, stay standing, and recover quickly. This chapter is about planning for failure. We'll explore how to keep systems running (high availability), how to switch to backups (site strategies), and how to practice for disaster (testing). For the Security+ exam, you need to think beyond prevention and into the realm of continuity—because a company that can't recover from an incident won't survive it.

**Security+ Exam Mindset**

This objective tests your knowledge of business continuity (BC) and disaster recovery (DR) concepts within a security context. You'll be given scenarios about outages, attacks, or disasters and asked to identify the correct resilience strategy (e.g., "Which site type should be used?"). Focus on the trade-offs: cost vs. recovery speed, simplicity vs. complexity. Understand the "why" behind each choice: Why use a hot site over a cold site? Why perform tabletop exercises?

## Section 1: Staying Online – High Availability & Redundancy

**High Availability (HA)**

- **Goal:** To ensure systems are operational and accessible for a very high percentage of the time (e.g., 99.999% or "five nines"). HA is about minimizing downtime.
- How it's achieved: Through redundancy—having multiple, redundant components so that if one fails, another takes over seamlessly.

### Load Balancing vs. Clustering

- **Load Balancing:** Distributes incoming network traffic or application requests across multiple servers. **Purpose:** Prevents any single server from being overwhelmed, improves performance, and provides fault tolerance. If one server fails, the load balancer stops sending traffic to it.
  - **Real-World Example:** A popular website uses a load balancer to send your request to one of ten identical web servers.
- **Clustering:** A group of servers (nodes) that work together as a single system. They share storage and are managed by clustering software. If one node fails, its workload is automatically transferred to another node (failover).
  - **Key Difference:** Clustering is typically a tighter integration for critical applications (like databases), while load balancing is often for scalable, stateless services (like web servers).

## Section 2: The Backup Plan – Site Considerations

### Site Considerations

When your primary location is down, where do you go?

- **Hot Site:** A fully configured, fully operational duplicate of your primary site, with live data synchronization. **Recovery Time Objective (RTO):** Minutes to hours. **Cost:** Very high.
  - **When to use:** For mission-critical operations where any downtime costs millions (e.g., stock trading floor).
- **Warm Site:** Has hardware and software installed, but data is not fully synchronized. May need recent backups restored and configurations updated. **RTO:** Several hours to 24 hours. **Cost:** Moderate.
  - **When to use:** A practical balance for most critical business functions.
- **Cold Site:** A facility with basic infrastructure (power, cooling, racks) but no pre-installed hardware or software. Everything must be delivered and set up. **RTO:** Days to weeks. **Cost:** Low.
  - **When to use:** For non-critical functions or as a long-term recovery option.
- **Geographic Dispersion:** Ensuring your primary and recovery sites are far enough apart that they won't be affected by the same regional disaster (hurricane, earthquake, flood). A nearby hot site is ineffective if the entire city floods.

## Section 3: Strategic Diversity

### Platform Diversity & Multi-Cloud Systems

- **Platform Diversity:** Using different types of technology (e.g., Windows and Linux servers, Cisco and Juniper firewalls). **Purpose:** Avoids single points of failure from a vendor-specific vulnerability. If a zero-day hits all Windows servers, your Linux servers may still operate.
- **Multi-Cloud:** Using more than one cloud service provider (e.g., AWS and Azure). **Purpose:** Prevents vendor lock-in and mitigates the risk of a total outage from a single CSP's regional failure. **Challenge:** Increases complexity and cost.

### Continuity of Operations (COOP)

- **The overarching goal:** The ability to continue essential functions during and after a disaster. It's thc "business" plan that DR and BC support.

## Section 4: Planning and Practice

### Capacity Planning

You must plan for the resources needed to recover and run in a degraded or alternate state.

- **People:** Do you have staff trained to operate the recovery site? Is there a call tree?
- **Technology:** Does your backup/recovery site have enough servers, bandwidth, and licenses?
- **Infrastructure:** Is there enough power, cooling, and physical space?

### Testing: The Only Way to Know if Your Plan Works

- **Tabletop Exercise:** A discussion-based session where key personnel walk through a simulated disaster scenario, talking through roles, responsibilities, and procedures. Cheap and effective for finding planning gaps.
- **Simulation:** A more hands-on test where systems are actually stressed or failed in a controlled manner, but without impacting production.
- **Failover Test:** The process of actually switching operations from the primary system to the backup system to ensure it works.
- **Parallel Processing:** Running the backup system simultaneously with the primary for testing, comparing outputs. Thorough but complex and costly.

## Section 5: The Lifeline – Backups & Data Recovery

### Data Backups & Data Recovery

Backups are the cornerstone of recovery. How you manage them determines if you can recover at all.

- **On-site vs. Off-site:**
    - **On-site:** Fast to restore, but vulnerable to the same disaster that hits the primary site (fire, theft).
    - **Off-site:** Protected from local disasters, but slower to retrieve. **Modern Solution:** Cloud backups serve as secure, geographically dispersed off-site storage.
- **The 3-2-1 Backup Rule:** A best practice. Have *three* total copies of your data, on *two* different media types, with *one* copy stored off-site.
- **Frequency & Recovery Point Objective (RPO):** How often you back up determines how much data you're willing to lose. With nightly backups, you could lose up to a day's work. Real-time replication means minimal data loss.
- **Encryption:** Backups must be encrypted, especially off-site or cloud backups, to protect data confidentiality.
- **Snapshots vs. Backups:**
    - **Snapshot:** A point-in-time *image* of a system (often a VM or database). Very fast to create and revert to, but usually stored on the same primary storage system. Not a true backup if the storage array fails.
- **Replication:** Real-time or near-real-time copying of data to another location. Used for hot sites and high availability. Ensures a very low RPO.
- **Journaling:** A logging technique (used in databases and filesystems) where changes are recorded in a log before being committed. Allows for recovery to a specific point in time, minimizing corruption.

## Section 6: Keeping the Lights On – Power

- **Uninterruptible Power Supply (UPS):** A battery backup that provides short-term, immediate power (minutes to hours) during an outage, allowing for a graceful shutdown of systems or time for generators to start.
- **Generators:** Provide ***long-term power*** (days) during extended outages. They take a few moments to start, which is why a UPS is always used in conjunction to bridge the gap.

# Chapter Summary

Resilience and recovery transform security from a binary "safe/breached" state to a spectrum of readiness. It's about designing for failure:

- **To stay up:** Use High Availability (load balancers, clustering) and geographic dispersion.
- **To recover:** Have a site strategy (hot/warm/cold) matched to your RTO and tested backups following the 3-2-1 rule.
- **To prepare:** Conduct capacity planning and regular tests (tabletops, simulations).
- **To endure:** Ensure platform diversity, multi-cloud strategies, and reliable power (UPS/generators).

The importance? *Business survival.* A ransomware attack that encrypts your data is an inconvenience if you have tested, isolated backups. It's a company-ending event if you don't.

**Exam-Related Tips**

1. **Hot, Warm, and Cold Sites:** Know the RTO and cost trade-off. **Hot = Fast/Expensive, Cold = Slow/Cheap.**
2. **Load Balancer = Scalability & Fault Tolerance. Clustering = High Availability for critical apps.**
3. **Backups must be encrypted and tested.** An untested backup is not a backup.
4. **UPS = Short-term bridge to generator.** Generator = Long-term power.
5. **Tabletop Exercise = Discussion-based, cheap, finds plan flaws.**

**Think Like the Exam**

*Scenario: "Following a major hurricane, a company's primary data center is offline. The company needs to restore its email and CRM systems within 8 hours to continue business operations. Management wants to minimize capital expenditure. Which recovery site type is MOST appropriate?"*

- **Requirement:** Restore within 8 hours (RTO < 1 day). Minimize cost.
- A **Hot Site** would meet the time requirement, but is too expensive (high CapEx).
- A **Cold Site** is cheap but too slow (takes days to set up).
- A **Warm Site** (with hardware pre-staged but data needing restoration) typically has an RTO of hours to a day and a moderate cost. *This is the best fit.*

**Self-Reflection Prompt**

Think about your most important digital asset (e.g., your phone photos, a project thesis). What is your *personal* resilience and recovery plan for it? Do you have backups? Are they off-site (cloud)? How often? How would you recover if your device were lost/stolen today? This personalizes the critical business concepts of RPO, RTO, and backup strategies.

# Domain 4:
# Security Operations

# Chapter 14 – The Daily Grind: Hardening and Securing Resources

## Exam Objective 4.1: Given a scenario, apply common security techniques to computing resources

*Chapter Introduction*

Welcome to the frontline of cybersecurity: **Security Operations (SecOps)**. This is where the policies and architectures meet reality. It's the day-to-day work of making systems *actually* secure. This chapter is your field manual for hardening: the process of stripping away unnecessary features, tightening configurations, and locking down everything from a server to a smartwatch. You'll learn how to establish a secure baseline, apply it across different targets (workstations, cloud, IoT), and manage the unique challenges of mobile and wireless devices. For the Security+ exam, you need to know the *specific actions* to take for each resource type and the *operational concepts* that keep them secure over time.

**Security+ Exam Mindset**

This is a highly practical, scenario-driven objective. CompTIA will describe a specific device or environment (e.g., "a new fleet of IoT sensors," "a cloud VM," "a corporate Wi-Fi network") and ask you to select the correct hardening step or security technique. You must move from the general principle ("harden the device") to the specific action ("disable unused ports, change default credentials"). Focus on the *"how"* and the *"what"* for each target.

## Section 1: The Foundation – Secure Baselines

A secure baseline is a standardized, secure configuration for a system or software.

**Establish, Deploy, Maintain**

1. **Establish:** Create the baseline. This is done by:
    - Using vendor security guidelines (CIS Benchmarks, DISA STIGs, Microsoft Security Baselines).
    - Defining configuration settings (disable services, set password policies, configure firewalls).

2. **Deploy:** Apply the baseline to systems. Methods include:
   - Group Policy Objects (GPO) for Windows domains.
   - Configuration management tools (Ansible, Puppet, Chef) for automated, consistent deployment.
   - Golden Images for virtual machines and containers.
3. **Maintain:** The ongoing process. Use SCAP (Security Content Automation Protocol) tools to scan systems for configuration drift (unauthorized changes from the baseline) and automatically remediate them.

**Why it Matters:** Baselines ensure consistency and compliance. Every system starts from a known, secure state.

## Section 2: The Targets – Hardening Specific Resources

Hardening steps vary by target, but follow the principle: *Minimize the attack surface.*

**Hardening Common Targets:**

- **Workstations/Servers:** Disable unnecessary services (e.g., Telnet, SMBv1), apply patches, enable host-based firewall/IPS, remove admin rights from standard users, implement application allow lists.
- **Switches/Routers:** Disable unused ports, change default credentials, enable port security (802.1X), use secure management protocols (SSH, disable Telnet/HTTP), and disable CDP/LLDP if not needed.
- **Cloud Infrastructure:** Apply the CSP's well-architected framework. Use identity and access management (IAM) with least privilege, encrypt data at rest, enable logging/monitoring (CloudTrail, Azure Monitor), and restrict security group (firewall) rules.
- **ICS/SCADA, Embedded, RTOS, IoT:** The challenge here is the inability to patch and the availability over security. Focus on network segmentation (air-gap or firewall zone), disable any network services not absolutely required, change default credentials (critical), and use virtual patching via an IPS to shield known vulnerabilities.

## Section 3: Taming the Airwaves – Wireless & Mobile

### Wireless Installation & Security

- **Site Surveys & Heat Maps:** Conducted before deployment to identify optimal access point (AP) placement, avoid interference, and ensure adequate coverage (eliminating dead zones where users might connect to rogue APs). A heat map visually shows signal strength.
- **Wireless Security Settings:**
    - **WPA3: Always the current standard.** Use WPA3-Enterprise (with 802.1X/RADIUS) for corporations. WPA3-Personal uses Simultaneous Authentication of Equals (SAE) to resist password cracking.
    - **AAA/RADIUS:** The enterprise solution for Wi-Fi. Provides central authentication, authorization, and accounting. Each user gets unique credentials.
    - **Avoid:** WEP, WPA, WPA2 (if WPA3 is available). TKIP is deprecated.

### Mobile Device Management (MDM) & Deployment Models

- **Mobile Device Management (MDM):** Software used to enforce security policies on mobile devices (smartphones, tablets).
    - **Capabilities:** Enforce passcodes, remotely wipe devices, enforce encryption, control app installation (allow lists), segment corporate data.
- **Deployment Models:**
    - **Corporate-Owned, Personally Enabled (COPE):** The company owns the device and allows some personal use. *Highest control.*
    - **Choose Your Own Device (CYOD):** Employee chooses from a pre-approved list of company-managed devices.
    - **Bring Your Own Device (BYOD):** Employee uses their personal device for work. *Highest risk.* MDM is used to create a secure container for corporate data only.

### Connection Methods & Security

- **Cellular:** Generally more secure than public Wi-Fi due to carrier encryption. Beware of SIM swapping attacks.
- **Wi-Fi:** Use VPN on untrusted networks. MDM can enforce this.
- **Bluetooth:** Use the latest versions, disable when not in use, and set to non-discoverable mode to avoid Bluejacking/Bluesnarfing.

## Section 4: Securing the Code – Application Security

- **Input Validation:** The #1 defense against **injection attacks** (SQLi, XSS). Check and sanitize *all* user input on the server side.
- **Secure Cookies:** Cookies should have the Secure flag (sent only over HTTPS) and the HttpOnly flag (inaccessible to JavaScript to prevent XSS theft).
- **Static Code Analysis (SAST):** Automated testing of source code for security vulnerabilities during the development phase ("shift left").
- **Code Signing:** Using a digital certificate to sign application code. Verifies the author and ensures the code hasn't been tampered with after publication.

## Section 5: Containment & Awareness

**Sandboxing**

- **What it is:** Running an application or process in an isolated, restricted environment to limit its access to the host system.
- **Purpose:** Containment. If the application is malicious or gets compromised, the damage is limited to the sandbox. Used in browsers (tab isolation), email attachments, and malware analysis.

**Monitoring**

- The continuous, operational practice of watching systems for signs of compromise, performance issues, or policy violations.
- Ties directly to Objective 2.4 (Indicators of Malicious Activity). You harden a system, then you monitor it to ensure it stays secure and to detect attacks that bypass your defenses.

# Chapter Summary

Securing computing resources is an operational discipline with a common workflow:

1. Start with a Secure Baseline for each type of resource.
2. Harden the Target with specific actions:
    - **Standard IT:** Disable services, patch, and use host-based controls.
    - **Specialized (IoT/ICS):** Segment, change defaults, use virtual patching.
    - **Wireless:** Use WPA3/802.1X, conduct site surveys.
    - **Mobile:** Enforce policy via MDM based on the deployment model (COPE, CYOD, BYOD).
3. Secure the Applications with input validation, code analysis, and signing.
4. Contain Risk with sandboxing.
5. Verify and Maintain through continuous monitoring and configuration drift checks.

The goal of operations is to turn architectural plans into a consistent, enforceable, and monitored reality.

**Exam-Related Tips**

1. **Baseline = CIS Benchmarks / STIGs.** Deployment = **GPO / Configuration Management.**
2. **IoT/ICS Hardening:** Focus is on **network segmentation and default passwords.** Patching is often not an option.
3. **WPA3 is the answer** for modern Wi-Fi security. **RADIUS** is for enterprise.
4. **MDM** is the solution for controlling corporate data on **BYOD** phones.
5. **Input Validation** is the direct mitigation for **SQLi and XSS.**

**Think Like the Exam**

*Scenario: "A company is deploying a new fleet of smart HVAC controllers (IoT devices) across its offices. The devices run a lightweight OS and connect to the corporate network for management. Which of the following hardening techniques is MOST critical to implement FIRST?"*

- The devices are IoT, on the corporate network.
- They likely have default credentials and an inability to patch.

- While segmentation is vital, the very first step before even connecting them is to change the default manufacturer passwords. This is the lowest-hanging fruit for any attacker scanning for IoT devices.
- **Correct Answer: Change default credentials.** Followed immediately by placing them on a dedicated, segmented network zone.

**Self-Reflection Prompt**

Pick a device you own (router, smart speaker, laptop). List 3 hardening steps you could take right now to make it more secure. Now, think about how a company would manage 10,000 of those devices. What operational tool (like MDM or configuration management) would they need? This bridges personal security to enterprise-scale operations.

# Chapter 15 – Knowing What You Have: Asset Management Security

## Exam Objective 4.2: Explain the security implications of proper hardware, software, and data asset management

*Chapter Introduction*

You can't secure what you don't know you have. An unknown server is an unpatched server. An unaccounted-for laptop is a data breach waiting to happen. Asset management is the unglamorous, foundational security discipline of knowing every piece of hardware, software, and data in your organization, from cradle to grave. This chapter walks through the lifecycle of an asset: how you acquire it, how you track it, how you classify the data on it, and finally, how you dispose of it securely. For the Security+ exam, you must understand that poor asset management is a root cause of security failures and that each stage of the lifecycle has critical security decisions attached to it.

**Security+ Exam Mindset**

This objective tests your understanding of process and consequence. CompTIA will ask questions about what happens when steps are skipped. For example: "What security risk is introduced by not maintaining a software inventory?" or "Which process ensures data is not recoverable from a decommissioned hard drive?" You need to connect the operational process (e.g., disposal) to the security goal (e.g., confidentiality).

## Section 1: The Beginning – Secure Acquisition & Procurement

**Acquisition/Procurement Process**

- **What it is:** The process of purchasing and introducing new hardware, software, or cloud services into the organization.
- **Security Implications:** This is the first point of risk introduction. A flawed process can bring in vulnerable devices, untrustworthy software, or non-compliant cloud services.
- **Key Security Actions:**

- **Vendor Risk Assessment:** Evaluating the security practices of the vendor before purchase.
- **Security Requirements in Contracts:** Mandating security features, support timelines, and breach notification terms.
- **Review for Compliance:** Ensuring the asset complies with relevant regulations (e.g., data sovereignty for cloud services).

**Real-World Example:** Purchasing network cameras? The procurement process should require that they do not "phone home" to unauthorized foreign countries and that they support changing default credentials.

## Section 2: Taking Ownership – Assignment & Classification

### Ownership & Classification

- **Ownership:** Assigning a person or team (the "data owner" or "system owner") who is accountable for the security and proper use of an asset. The owner is responsible for classifying its data and authorizing access.
- **Classification:** The process of categorizing data based on its sensitivity (e.g., Public, Confidential, Restricted) as defined in Objective 3.3.
- **Security Implications:**
  - **Without clear ownership,** security responsibilities are diffused, and no one is accountable. Assets become "orphaned."
  - **Without classification,** you cannot apply appropriate security controls. You end up either over-protecting public data (wasting resources) or under-protecting secrets (creating risk).

**The Link:** The **owner** is responsible for determining the classification. This drives all subsequent security controls (encryption, access permissions, retention policies).

## Section 3: The Watchful Eye – Monitoring & Asset Tracking

### Inventory & Enumeration

- **Inventory:** A comprehensive **Correct Answer** inventory includes make, model, serial number, location, and owner. Software inventory includes title, version, and license.
- **Enumeration:** The technical process of actively discovering assets on the network (using tools like network scanners, vulnerability scanners, or agent-based systems).

- **Security Implications:**
  - **Visibility:** You cannot patch, monitor, or secure an asset you don't know exists. Unknown assets are blind spots for attackers to hide in.
  - **Vulnerability Management:** A software inventory is essential for knowing what needs to be patched. An out-of-date inventory leads to unpatched, exploitable systems.
  - **Compliance:** Many regulations (like PCI DSS) require you to maintain an accurate asset inventory.

## Section 4: The Secure End – Disposal & Decommissioning

This phase is about ensuring that retired assets do not become a source of data leaks.

**Sanitization vs. Destruction**

- **Sanitization:** Making data on the media unrecoverable by software or laboratory techniques. The media can be reused.
  - **Methods:** Clear (overwriting with 0s/1s), Purge (degaussing magnetic media), Cryptographic Erase (deleting the encryption key).
- **Destruction:** Physically damaging the media so it cannot be reused or data recovered.
  - **Methods:** Shredding, pulverizing, incinerating, drilling.

**Data Retention & Certification**

- **Data Retention Policies:** Legal or business rules that define how long data must be kept before it is eligible for secure disposal. Keeping data longer than required increases liability; deleting it too soon can violate laws.
- **Certification:** The formal documentation that sanitization or destruction was performed according to policy. This provides an audit trail for compliance (e.g., a certificate of destruction from a shredding service).

**Real-World Example:** A hospital decommissioning old laptops used for patient records must:

1. Follow its data retention policy to ensure records are kept for the legally required period (e.g., 7 years).
2. Perform sanitization (cryptographic erase if FDE was used, or a secure wipe).
3. Obtain a certificate of sanitization for its audit logs.
4. Then, the hardware can be destroyed or remarketed.

**The Security Implications of Poor Asset Management**

| Lifecycle Stage | If Skipped or Done Poorly... | Resulting Security Risk |
|---|---|---|
| **Acquisition** | No security review of vendor/software. | Introduction of vulnerable, backdoored, or non-compliant assets. |
| **Assignment** | No clear owner. | Lack of accountability. No one classifies data or authorizes access. |
| **Classification** | Data is not classified. | Inconsistent protection. Secrets may have weak controls; public data may be over-restricted. |
| **Inventory** | No accurate asset list. | Blind spots. Unpatched systems, unauthorized (shadow IT) systems, and rogue devices persist. |
| **Disposal** | No sanitization. | Data Breach. Sensitive data recovered from discarded drives, sold equipment, or recycled hardware. |

# Chapter Summary

Proper asset management is the operational backbone of information security. It's a continuous lifecycle:

1. Procure with security in mind.
2. Assign an owner and classify the data.
3. Track everything in an inventory.
4. Dispose securely based on retention policies, using sanitization/destruction, and certify the action.

The core security principle here is accountability and control. From the moment an asset enters the organization to the moment it is destroyed, you must know what it is, who is responsible for it, what it contains, and where it is. Failure at any point creates risk, waste, and compliance violations.

**Exam-Related Tips**

1. Inventory is for Visibility. It's the answer to "How do you ensure all systems are patched?"
2. Classification drives controls. It's the answer to "How do you determine what level of encryption to use?"
3. Sanitization = Data Unrecoverable. Destruction = Physical Demolition. Know the methods.
4. Certification is the audit proof that disposal was done correctly.
5. Data Retention Policies tell you when you can dispose of data. Disposing too early is a legal risk; too late is a security risk.

**Think Like the Exam**

*Scenario: "A company is retiring a fleet of 200 laptops used by its finance department. The IT manager suggests donating them to a local school after performing a standard operating system format. The Chief Information Security Officer (CISO) objects. Which of the following is the MOST likely reason for the CISO's objection?"*

- The laptops were used by the finance department, meaning they likely contain sensitive, confidential data.
- A standard OS format does not sanitize data. The files are marked as deleted, but the data remains physically on the drive and is easily recoverable with simple tools.

- The CISO objects because this disposal method does not prevent data recovery, creating a high risk of a data breach when the laptops are donated.
- The correct solution would be to perform data sanitization (e.g., a multi-pass wipe) or destruction of the drives before donation.

**Self-Reflection Prompt**

Take a mental inventory of your own digital assets: your laptop, phone, old hard drives in a drawer, cloud accounts. Who "owns" each one (you)? How is the data "classified" (e.g., personal photos vs. tax documents)? What is your "disposal plan" for your old phone? Do you just factory reset it, or do you take more secure steps? This personal audit makes the enterprise process relatable.

# Chapter 16 – The Vulnerability Lifecycle: Find, Fix, Verify

## Exam Objective 4.3:

## Explain various activities associated with vulnerability management

*Chapter Introduction*

Vulnerabilities are the cracks in your digital armor. Vulnerability management is the continuous, cyclical process of finding those cracks, figuring out which ones are most dangerous, fixing them, and making sure they stay fixed. It's not a one-time scan; it's an ongoing program that's central to proactive security. This chapter breaks down the entire workflow: from the tools that identify weaknesses (scanners, threat feeds, pentests) to the framework used to analyze and prioritize them (CVSS), and finally, the operations to remediate and validate the fixes. For the Security+ exam, you need to understand the purpose and output of each stage in the cycle.

**Security+ Exam Mindset**

This objective requires you to sequence activities and understand outputs. CompTIA will ask things like: "What is the purpose of a dynamic analysis?" or "After a vulnerability scan, what should be done next?" or "What does a CVSS score of 9.8 indicate?" You must understand the vulnerability management pipeline from start to finish.

## Section 1: The Hunt – Identification Methods

How do you find vulnerabilities? You use a mix of automated tools and human intelligence.

**Vulnerability Scan**

- **What it is:** An automated, non-intrusive process that uses a database of known vulnerabilities (fingerprints, version checks) to identify potential weaknesses on systems, networks, or applications.
- **Output:** A list of potential vulnerabilities, often with a severity rating. It's a broad net that catches known issues.
- **Key Point:** It can produce false positives (saying a vulnerability exists when it doesn't) and false negatives (missing a real vulnerability).

**Application Security Testing**

- **Static Application Security Testing (SAST):** Analyzing source code for vulnerabilities *before* the application is run ("white-box" testing). Finds issues like insecure functions and logic flaws early in the SDLC.
- **Dynamic Application Security Testing (DAST):** Analyzing a running application from the outside ("black-box" testing). Finds runtime issues like configuration errors and vulnerabilities visible in HTTP responses.
- **Package Monitoring/Software Composition Analysis (SCA):** Scanning application dependencies and libraries (like those from npm, Maven) for known vulnerabilities. Critical because most modern apps are built on third-party code.

**Threat Feeds & Intelligence**

- **Open-Source Intelligence (OSINT):** Publicly available information about threats (security blogs, vendor advisories, CVE lists).
- **Proprietary/Third-Party Feeds:** Commercial or curated feeds that provide timely, actionable threat intelligence.
- **Information-Sharing Organizations:** Sector-specific groups (like ISACs) where companies share anonymized threat data.
- **Dark Web Monitoring:** Scanning underground forums and markets for mentions of your company, stolen data, or exploit sales.
- **Purpose:** These feeds help you understand the threat landscape and prioritize vulnerabilities that are being actively exploited in the wild.

**Penetration Testing**

- **What it is:** A simulated, authorized cyberattack performed by ethical hackers to exploit vulnerabilities and assess the security of a system.
- **Key Difference from Vulnerability Scanning:** Pentesting is manual, intrusive, and goal-oriented (e.g., "can you breach the database?"). It validates findings and demonstrates impact. A scan *identifies*; a pentest *exploits*.

**Responsible Disclosure & Bug Bounty**

- **Responsible Disclosure Program:** A formal channel for external security researchers to **safely report** vulnerabilities they find in your systems.

- **Bug Bounty Program:** A monetized responsible disclosure program that pays researchers for valid vulnerabilities. Incentivizes finding bugs before criminals do.

**System/Process Audit**

- A manual review of systems, configurations, and processes against a security standard or baseline (e.g., checking if password policies are correctly implemented). Finds misconfigurations that scanners might miss.

## Section 2: Making Sense of It All – Analysis

You have a list of findings. Now you must triage them.

**Confirmation & Prioritization**

- **Confirmation:** Manually verifying scan results to weed out false positives. A critical step before wasting effort on non-issues.
- **False Negative:** A vulnerability that exists but was not detected. More dangerous than a false positive.
- **Prioritization:** You can't fix everything at once. You must rank vulnerabilities based on risk.

**The Prioritization Framework: CVSS & CVE**

- **Common Vulnerability Enumeration (CVE):** A standard identifier for a known vulnerability (e.g., CVE-2021-44228 for Log4Shell). It's just a name/number.
- **Common Vulnerability Scoring System (CVSS):** A standard scoring system (0.0-10.0) that reflects the severity of a vulnerability.
    - **Base Score:** Intrinsic qualities of the vulnerability (how easy to exploit, what impact).
    - **Temporal Score:** Changes over time (is there a patch? is there exploit code?).
    - **Environmental Score:** Adjusted for your specific environment (how critical is the affected system to *you*?).
- **A CVSS score of 9.0-10.0 is CRITICAL** and should be patched immediately.

**Risk-Based Factors**

- **Exposure Factor:** What percentage of an asset would be lost if the vulnerability was exploited?

- **Environmental Variables:** How is the vulnerable system used in *your* organization?
- **Industry/Organizational Impact:** A vulnerability in a hospital's patient system has higher real-world impact than the same vulnerability in a gaming company's test server.
- **Risk Tolerance:** How much risk is the organization willing to accept? This business decision dictates what gets fixed and what gets accepted or transferred.

## Section 3: Taking Action – Response & Remediation

### Remediation Actions

- **Patching:** The ideal fix. Applying a vendor update to eliminate the vulnerability.
- **Compensating Controls:** If you can't patch immediately (e.g., legacy system), implement a control that reduces risk. Example: Use a network firewall or IPS to block exploit traffic (virtual patching).
- **Segmentation:** Isolate the vulnerable system to limit the potential blast radius if exploited.
- **Insurance:** Risk transference. Cybersecurity insurance can help offset financial losses from an exploited vulnerability, but it doesn't fix the hole.

### Exceptions & Exemptions

- A formal, documented, and time-bound approval to not remediate a vulnerability due to a business or technical constraint (e.g., "This patch breaks our legacy manufacturing software; exemption granted for 60 days while a fix is developed."). Must be reviewed and approved by management/security.

## Section 4: Closing the Loop – Validation & Reporting

The job isn't done until you prove it's fixed.

### Validation of Remediation

- **Rescanning:** Running the vulnerability scan again on the affected system to confirm the finding is gone.
- **Audit:** Checking change logs or system configurations to verify the patch was applied.
- **Verification:** Manual testing to ensure the fix works and doesn't break functionality.

### Reporting

- Communicating the entire process and its outcomes to stakeholders. Reports include:
    - Vulnerabilities found.
    - Risk ratings (CVSS).

    - Remediation actions taken.
    - Metrics (time to patch, number of open critical vulnerabilities).
    - Status of exceptions.
- **Purpose:** Demonstrates the effectiveness of the vulnerability management program, informs decision-makers, and satisfies compliance requirements.

# Chapter Summary

Vulnerability management is a continuous, four-phase cycle:

1. **IDENTIFY** using scans, pentests, threat intel, and audits.
2. **ANALYZE** to confirm findings, eliminate false positives, and prioritize using CVSS and business context.
3. **REMEDIATE** by patching, implementing compensating controls, or formally accepting risk via exceptions.
4. **VALIDATE & REPORT** by rescanning, verifying fixes, and communicating results.

The goal is not to have zero vulnerabilities (impossible), but to manage risk by ensuring the most critical weaknesses are addressed in a timely manner, based on their likelihood of exploitation and potential impact on your business.

**Exam-Related Tips**

1. **Scan = Automated, Non-Intrusive List. Pentest = Manual, Intrusive Exploitation.**
2. **SAST = Source Code. DAST = Running App.**
3. **CVE = Name. CVSS = Score.** A high CVSS (e.g., 9.8) = patch immediately.
4. **Compensating Control** is the answer when you cannot patch (e.g., legacy system).
5. **Validation = Rescanning.** You must prove the fix worked.
6. **Exceptions are formal, documented, and temporary.**

**Think Like the Exam**

*Scenario: "A vulnerability scan identifies a critical remote code execution flaw (CVSS 9.1) on an internet-facing web server. The server hosts a legacy application that cannot be patched without a six-month rewrite. Which of the following is the BEST immediate course of action?"*

- The vulnerability is critical (9.1) and on an internet-facing server (high exposure).
- Patching is impossible in the short term.
- The immediate goal is to reduce risk while a long-term fix is developed.
- The BEST action is to implement a compensating control. In this case, placing a Web Application Firewall (WAF) in front of the server to filter out exploit attempts ("virtual patching") or segmenting the server behind a stricter firewall would be appropriate. An

exception would be too risky for a critical, internet-facing flaw without any mitigating controls.

**Self-Reflection Prompt**

Think of an app on your phone. How would a vulnerability in that app be identified (hint: the vendor's SAST/DAST, or a bug bounty)? How would it be prioritized (CVSS based on what it can access)? What would the remediation be (an update pushed to your phone)? This connects the enterprise process to your personal tech updates.

# Chapter 17 – The Security Nerve Center: Alerting and Monitoring

## Exam Objective 4.4:

## Explain security alerting and monitoring concepts and tools

*Chapter Introduction*

Imagine your network is a city. Monitoring is the network of security cameras, motion sensors, and patrol logs. Alerting is the alarm that sounds when a camera spots a break-in. Without this continuous watchfulness, you'd never know you were under attack until it was too late. This chapter dives into the **Security Operations Center (SOC)** world—the 24/7 process of watching over systems, collecting logs, detecting anomalies, and responding to alerts. You'll learn *what* to monitor, *how* to collect the data, the *tools* that make sense of it all, and the *actions* to take when an alarm goes off. For the Security+ exam, you must understand that monitoring is not passive observation; it's an active, analytical process that drives incident response.

**Security+ Exam Mindset**

This objective blends concepts and tool knowledge. CompTIA will ask you to match a monitoring goal to a specific tool (e.g., "What provides centralized log aggregation and analysis?") or to identify the next step in an alert response workflow. You need to understand the purpose and output of each major tool (SIEM, DLP, NetFlow) and the operational activities that turn raw data into security intelligence.

## Section 1: What to Watch – Monitoring Targets

**Monitoring Computing Resources**

- **Systems:** Monitoring servers, workstations, endpoints for signs of compromise (unusual process activity, file changes, high CPU, failed logons).
- **Applications:** Monitoring software behavior for errors, crashes, unauthorized access attempts, and performance issues. Especially critical for web applications.
- **Infrastructure:** Monitoring network devices (switches, routers, firewalls) and cloud infrastructure (VMs, storage buckets, IAM) for configuration changes, availability, and suspicious traffic patterns.

**Principle:** You monitor the assets you identified in asset management. The goal is to establish a baseline of normal behavior so you can spot anomalies.

## Section 2: The Operational Cycle – Key Activities

**Log Aggregation & Archiving**

- **Log Aggregation:** The process of collecting logs from diverse sources (firewalls, servers, applications) and sending them to a central system (like a SIEM). This provides a single pane of glass for analysis.
- **Archiving:** Storing logs for long-term retention to meet compliance requirements (often 7+ years) and for forensic analysis if an incident is discovered long after it occurred.

**Alerting & Scanning**

- **Alerting:** Automated notifications triggered when a monitoring system detects a predefined condition or anomaly (e.g., "10 failed logins in 1 minute," "outbound connection to known malicious IP").
- **Scanning:** Proactive activity. Regularly scheduled vulnerability scans and configuration compliance checks (using tools like SCAP) to find weaknesses *before* they are exploited.

**Reporting**

- Generating summaries of security status, events, and trends for management and auditors. Reports answer questions like: "How many critical alerts did we have this month?" "Are we meeting our patching SLAs?"

**Alert Response & Remediation/Validation**

This is where monitoring meets action.

1. **Quarantine:** An immediate containment action. Isolating a compromised system from the network to prevent the threat from spreading.
2. **Alert Tuning:** The process of refining alert rules to reduce false positives (noisy alerts that waste time) and minimize false negatives (missed real threats). This is a continuous improvement task.
3. **Remediation/Validation:** Fixing the root cause (e.g., patching, removing malware) and then validating that the fix worked and the system is clean (rescanning, re-imaging).

## Section 3: The Toolbox – Key Monitoring Tools

### Security Content Automation Protocol (SCAP) & Benchmarks

- **SCAP:** A suite of standards that allow for automated vulnerability scanning, configuration checking, and compliance reporting. It uses benchmarks like CIS Benchmarks or DISA STIGs as the secure configuration standard.
- **Benchmarks:** The checklists that SCAP tools use. They define the secure settings for an OS or application.

### Agents vs. Agentless Monitoring

- **Agent-Based:** A small software program (agent) is installed on the system being monitored. It collects detailed data (process info, file integrity) and sends it to a manager. More powerful but requires deployment/maintenance.
- **Agentless:** Monitoring performed remotely, often using credentials to log in and check settings (e.g., WMI for Windows, SSH for Linux). Easier to deploy but may collect less granular data.

### Core Security Tools

- **Security Information and Event Management (SIEM):** The brain of modern monitoring. It performs log aggregation, correlation (linking related events from different sources), analysis, and alerting. It's where you see "Alice's account logged in from New York and Moscow within 5 minutes."
- **Antivirus/Anti-Malware/EDR:** Endpoint monitoring and protection. Detects and blocks known malware signatures and, in the case of EDR (Endpoint Detection and Response), uses behavioral analysis to detect unknown threats.
- **Data Loss Prevention (DLP):** Monitors data in use, in transit, and at rest to detect and prevent unauthorized exfiltration of sensitive information (e.g., a user trying to email a file containing credit card numbers to a personal Gmail account).
- **Simple Network Management Protocol (SNMP) Traps:** Messages sent from network devices (routers, switches, UPS) to a management station to alert about events like a failed interface, high temperature, or fan error. Used for infrastructure health monitoring.
- **NetFlow/sFlow/IPFIX:** Network traffic analysis protocols. They provide metadata about network conversations (source/destination IP, port, protocol, bytes transferred) but not the content. Used to detect anomalies like data exfiltration, DDoS attacks, and unauthorized communications.

- **Vulnerability Scanners:** Tools (like Nessus, Qualys) that proactively scan networks and systems for known vulnerabilities and misconfigurations, as covered in Objective 4.3.

# Chapter Summary

Alerting and monitoring form the continuous feedback loop of security operations. It's a cycle of:

1. **Collection:** Aggregating logs and data from systems, apps, and infrastructure.
2. **Analysis:** Using tools like SIEM, NetFlow, and DLP to correlate data and find threats.
3. **Alerting:** Generating alerts based on rules and anomalies.
4. **Response:** Taking action (quarantine), tuning alerts, and remediating the issue.
5. **Validation & Reporting:** Ensuring the fix worked and documenting everything.

The goal is to achieve situational awareness—to know what's happening in your environment in near real time—and to enable a fast, effective response to incidents.

**Exam-Related Tips**

1. **SIEM = Centralized Log Aggregation, Correlation, and Alerting.** This is a key answer.
2. **DLP = Monitors for Sensitive Data Leaving.** Think "data exfiltration."
3. **NetFlow = Network Traffic Metadata Analysis.** Used for spotting data transfers to suspicious IPs.
4. **SCAP = Automated Compliance/Vulnerability Scanning** using Benchmarks.
5. **Alert Tuning = Reducing False Positives.** A critical SOC activity to avoid "alert fatigue."
6. **Quarantine = Immediate Containment Step** upon a high-confidence alert.

**Think Like the Exam**

*Scenario: "A SOC analyst sees an alert in the SIEM indicating that a workstation is sending gigabytes of data to an external IP address in a foreign country over port 443. The DLP system has not triggered. Which tool would have been the PRIMARY source of the metadata that generated this initial alert?"*

- The alert is about network traffic patterns (high volume to a foreign IP).
- The content of the traffic is encrypted (port 443/HTTPS), so DLP (which inspects content) didn't trigger.
- The SIEM correlated the event, but the source of the raw traffic metadata is likely a **NetFlow** exporter on the network router or switch that feeds data into the SIEM.
- **Correct Answer:** NetFlow.

**Self-Reflection Prompt**

Look at your own computer's activity monitor or task manager. That's a basic form of system monitoring. Now, imagine you're the SOC for your own digital life. What would you need to monitor? (e.g., login attempts, new software installs, outbound connections). What simple "alerts" would you want? (e.g., "New device logged into your email"). This builds the mindset of thinking about your own environment in monitoring terms.

# Chapter 18 – The Security Tuning Knobs: Modifying Enterprise Capabilities

## Exam Objective 4.5:
## Given a scenario, modify enterprise capabilities to enhance security

*Chapter Introduction*

Security isn't a "set it and forget it" project. It's a constant process of tuning and adjustment. You have your foundational tools in place—firewalls, IDS, and email gateways. Now, how do you make them smarter, sharper, and more effective? This chapter is about the advanced configuration and strategic modifications you make to these capabilities to proactively improve your security posture. Given a specific security gap or emerging threat (the scenario), you'll learn how to tweak rules, deploy new filtering layers, and implement protocols to close the gap. For the Security+ exam, you need to move beyond knowing *what* a tool is, to knowing *how to configure it* to solve a real problem.

**Security+ Exam Mindset**

This is a practical, configuration-focused objective. CompTIA will present a clear problem (e.g., "Too many phishing emails are reaching users," "Insiders are copying sensitive data to USB drives," "A new worm is spreading via SMB") and ask you to select the correct modification to an existing security capability. You must match the technical control to the specific symptom.

## Section 1: Network Traffic Control – Firewalls & Filtering

**Firewall Modifications**

To enhance security, you modify:

- **Rules & Access Control Lists (ACLs):** Apply the principle of least privilege. Change from permissive "allow any" rules to deny-by-default, only allowing necessary traffic. Regularly review and prune old rules.
- **Ports/Protocols: Disable unused ports/protocols** on firewall interfaces. If a business unit no longer uses FTP, block port 21. This reduces the attack surface.

- **Screened Subnets (DMZ):** Enhance security by modifying the architecture. Place public-facing servers in a DMZ with strict firewall rules that only allow specific traffic from the internet to the DMZ, and even stricter rules from the DMZ to the internal network.

**Scenario Application:** *"To prevent a new ransomware variant from communicating with its command-and-control server, you would add a firewall rule to* ***block outbound traffic*** *to the known malicious IP addresses and domains at the perimeter."*

**Web Filter Modifications**

- Agent-based vs. Centralized Proxy: Agent-based filtering enforces policy on managed devices anywhere. Centralized proxy forces all traffic through a chokepoint for inspection. Enhancing security might mean deploying agents to remote laptops.
- URL Scanning, Content Categorization & Block Rules: Enhance by adding new categories to block (e.g., "Cryptocurrency Mining," "Newly Registered Domains"), updating URL reputation databases, and creating custom block rules for specific phishing sites.
- Reputation Filtering: Block access to websites with poor reputation scores. Tune by adjusting reputation thresholds.

**Scenario Application:** *"To reduce infections from drive-by downloads, enhance the web filter to* ***block access to sites in the 'Malware' and 'High-Risk' categories*** *and to newly registered domains not yet categorized."*

**DNS Filtering**

- A lightweight but powerful capability. Modifying it to block DNS resolutions to known malicious domains, phishing sites, or unwanted content categories prevents users from even reaching bad sites, regardless of port or protocol.

## Section 2: Threat Detection – IDS/IPS & Endpoint

**IDS/IPS Modifications**

- **Signatures:** To detect a new threat, you must update the signature database. To reduce false positives, you tune or disable overly broad signatures.
- **Trends:** Use historical data to create baselines. Then, modify the IPS to alert on or block significant deviations from the baseline (anomaly-based detection).

**Scenario Application:** *"After a zero-day exploit is published, you would* ***ensure the IPS signature feed is updated*** *to the latest version to potentially obtain a new signature, and consider enabling more aggressive anomaly detection for the targeted service."*

**Endpoint Detection and Response (EDR) / Extended Detection and Response (XDR)**

- EDR focuses on endpoints. XDR integrates data from endpoints, network, cloud, and email for better correlation.
- **Enhancement:** Deploy EDR agents to all critical servers and workstations if not already done. Configure XDR to create correlation rules that, for example, link a phishing email alert from the gateway with a subsequent malicious process on an endpoint.

**User Behavior Analytics (UBA)**

- A **behavior-modification** capability. UBA establishes a baseline of normal user activity (logon times, files accessed, data volume). To enhance security, you create alerts for anomalous behavior, like a user downloading thousands of files they've never accessed before (potential data exfiltration) or logging in at 3 AM from a foreign country.

## Section 3: System & Data Security

**Operating System Security**

- **Group Policy (Windows):** The primary tool for enforcing secure baselines at scale. Enhance security by creating/modifying GPOs to disable USB storage, enforce password complexity, deploy software patches, or apply firewall settings.
- **SELinux (Linux):** A mandatory access control system. Enhance security by switching from "permissive" mode to "enforcing" mode and defining strict policies for what processes can access which files, ports, and directories.

**File Integrity Monitoring (FIM)**

- Tools that alert you to unauthorized changes to critical system files, configurations, or sensitive data. Enhance by expanding the scope of monitored files to include new applications, or by increasing the frequency of checks.

**Data Loss Prevention (DLP)**

- To enhance, you must refine your DLP policies. This includes:
    - Adding new sensitive data patterns (e.g., a new project code name).
    - Tuning detection rules to reduce false positives.
    - Expanding coverage to new channels (e.g., blocking uploads of source code to cloud storage).

## Section 4: Access & Communication Security

**Network Access Control (NAC)**

- Enhances security by controlling which devices can connect to the network. Modifications include:
  - Stricter posture checking (requiring antivirus to be active and updated).
  - Placing non-compliant or guest devices on a more restricted quarantine VLAN.

**Secure Protocol Implementation**

- **Protocol Selection:** Replace insecure protocols with secure ones. Modify systems to disable SSLv2/3, TLS 1.0/1.1, SMBv1, Telnet, FTP, and enable TLS 1.2/1.3, SSH, SFTP, SMBv3.
- **Port Selection:** Sometimes security through obscurity can be a layer; changing a service from a well-known port (e.g., SSH from 22 to 5022) can reduce noise from automated scanners.
- **Transport Method:** Mandate the use of VPNs for all remote access instead of direct RDP/SSH exposed to the internet.

**Email Security**

To combat phishing and spoofing, you enhance email authentication by deploying and correctly configuring:

- **Sender Policy Framework (SPF):** A DNS record that lists which mail servers are authorized to send email for your domain.
- **DomainKeys Identified Mail (DKIM):** Adds a digital signature to outgoing email, allowing the recipient to verify it came from your domain and wasn't altered.
- **Domain-based Message Authentication, Reporting & Conformance (DMARC):** A policy that uses SPF and DKIM results to tell receiving mail servers what to do with emails that fail authentication (e.g., quarantine or reject). DMARC reports are critical for tuning.
- **Gateway Filtering:** Enhance the email gateway by updating anti-spam/anti-phish engines, adding impersonation protection rules for executives, and blocking attachments with dangerous extensions (.scr, .js).

**Scenario Application:** *"To stop attackers from spoofing your CEO's email address, you would **implement SPF, DKIM, and a DMARC policy with a 'reject' directive** for your domain, and configure the email gateway to flag internal email coming from outside the organization."*

# Chapter Summary

Modifying enterprise capabilities is about active security management. It involves:

- **Tuning** existing tools (firewall rules, IDS signatures, web/DNS filters) to be more precise and effective.
- **Expanding** coverage (deploying EDR, enabling FIM on more systems).
- **Enforcing** standards (via Group Policy, NAC, secure protocols).
- **Layering** defenses (adding email authentication on top of gateway filtering).

The goal is to iteratively close gaps, reduce noise, and raise the cost for attackers by making your defenses more intelligent and adaptive.

**Exam-Related Tips**

1. DMARC/SPF/DKIM are the trio for preventing email spoofing. DMARC provides the policy and reporting.
2. Group Policy is the answer for enforcing Windows settings at scale.
3. NAC is for controlling device access based on compliance.
4. DLP is modified to protect new types of sensitive data.
5. To stop a specific threat, you update IDS/IPS signatures and firewall block lists.
6. UBA detects insider threats based on deviations from normal behavior.

**Think Like the Exam**

*Scenario: "A company is experiencing an increase in sophisticated phishing attacks where the emails appear to come from legitimate partner domains. The attackers are successfully spoofing the 'From' address. The company's current email gateway is missing many of these messages. Which of the following modifications would be MOST effective in reducing this threat?"*

- The problem is email spoofing from external domains.
- The gateway is missing them, so you need a different layer of defense.
- The gateway filters content, but it can't inherently verify if an email from partnername.com is actually from partner.com's real mail servers.
- The most effective modification is to implement and enforce DMARC policies for your own domain (to protect your brand) and advocate for your partners to do the same. However, for inbound mail, you can configure your email gateway to strictly enforce

DMARC checks on incoming mail and quarantine/reject messages that fail authentication from domains that publish DMARC records. This is a modification of the gateway's authentication checking capabilities.

**Self-Reflection Prompt**

Think of your home Wi-Fi router. It has basic capabilities (a firewall, Wi-Fi settings). List 2-3 modifications you could make to enhance its security (e.g., change default password, disable WPS, enable WPA3, create a guest network). This is the exact same concept of modifying an enterprise capability, just at a smaller scale.

# Chapter 19 – The Gatekeepers: Implementing Identity and Access Management (IAM)

## Exam Objective 4.6:
## Given a scenario, implement and maintain identity and access management

*Chapter Introduction*

Identity is the new security perimeter. In a world of cloud apps, remote work, and mobile devices, the old castle walls are gone. The core question is: *"Who are you, and what are you allowed to do?"* **Identity and Access Management (IAM)** is the comprehensive answer. This chapter covers the entire lifecycle of digital identity—from creating an account (provisioning) to proving who you are (authentication) to defining what you can access (authorization), and finally, removing access when it's no longer needed (de-provisioning). For the Security+ exam, you must understand hands-on implementation of these concepts: configuring SSO, enforcing least privilege, deploying MFA, and managing privileged accounts. Given a scenario, you'll need to select the correct IAM control to solve a security or operational problem.

**Security+ Exam Mindset**

This is a deeply practical and scenario-heavy objective. CompTIA will describe an access-related problem (e.g., "Users have too many permissions," "We need to integrate cloud app logins," "How do we secure admin accounts?") and ask you to choose the appropriate IAM solution. You must know the differences between federation protocols (SAML vs. OAuth), the types of access controls, and the mechanics of MFA and password management.

## Section 1: The Identity Lifecycle – Provisioning to De-provisioning

**Provisioning & De-provisioning**

- **Provisioning:** The process of creating and configuring a user account and granting the initial set of permissions needed to perform a job.
- **De-provisioning:** The process of removing or disabling access when a user leaves the organization or changes roles.

- **Security Implications:** Orphaned accounts (not de-provisioned) are a major risk—they belong to ex-employees and are unmonitored, perfect for attackers. Automated provisioning/de-provisioning (e.g., linked to HR systems) is a best practice to ensure timeliness.

**Identity Proofing**

- Verifying that a person is who they claim to be before issuing credentials. This is the "trust but verify" step for initial account creation.
- **Methods:** In-person with government ID, video call with document verification, knowledge-based verification (answering personal questions from credit history).

## Section 2: Authorization – Defining Permissions

**Permission Assignments & Implications**

- **Assignments:** Granting specific rights (Read, Write, Execute) to resources (files, shares, applications).
- **Implications:** The principle of least privilege must guide assignments. Users should only get permissions essential for their role. Over-provisioning creates excessive risk.

**Access Control Models (Review from Objective 1.2, now with implementation focus)**

- **Mandatory Access Control (MAC):** Implemented via security labels (Top Secret, Confidential). The *system* enforces policy. Used in government/military.
- **Discretionary Access Control (DAC)**: Implemented via file/folder permissions where the *owner* controls access. Common in consumer OS.
- **Role-Based Access Control (RBAC):** Implemented by creating groups (e.g., "Finance_Team," "Helpdesk_Admins") and assigning permissions to the group, not individual users. Users are added to groups based on their role. Most common in enterprises.
- **Attribute-Based Access Control (ABAC):** Implemented using policies that evaluate multiple attributes (user department + file classification + time of day). More granular but complex. (e.g., "Allow access to the budget file IF user is in Finance AND it's a weekday 9-5.")
- **Time-of-Day Restrictions:** A simple rule-based control. Implemented in NAC systems or Active Directory to block logins outside of business hours for certain users.

## Section 3: Modern Access – Federation & Single Sign-On (SSO)

**Federation & SSO**

- **Federation:** A trust relationship between two organizations that allows users from one (the Identity Provider - IdP) to access resources in another (the Service Provider - SP) using their existing credentials.
- **Single Sign-On (SSO):** A user authenticates once to the IdP and gains access to multiple, related but independent software systems (SPs) without logging in again.

**Key Protocols (Know the Difference!)**

- **Lightweight Directory Access Protocol (LDAP):** A directory services protocol used to query and manage user accounts in a directory (like Active Directory). It's for authentication and user lookup, not typically for web SSO.
- **Security Assertions Markup Language (SAML):** An XML-based standard for web browser SSO. The user wants to access a cloud app (SP), is redirected to the company IdP (like Okta, Azure AD) to log in, and the IdP sends a SAML assertion (a signed digital token) back to the app saying "this user is authenticated." Common in enterprise-to-cloud SSO.
- **Open Authorization (OAuth 2.0):** An authorization framework, not primarily for authentication. It allows a user to grant a third-party application limited access to their resources (e.g., "Allow 'FitnessApp' to read your Google profile"). OAuth provides ***delegated access.*** It's the "Log in with Google/Facebook" button.
- **OpenID Connect (OIDC):** A simple identity layer built on top of OAuth 2.0. It adds an ID Token (a JWT) to standard OAuth flows to provide authentication information. OIDC is for *authentication*. Modern web/mobile apps often use OIDC.

**Implementation Scenario:** To allow employees to log into Salesforce using their corporate AD credentials, you would implement SAML-based SSO, where your AD acts as the IdP.

**Interoperability & Attestation**

- **Interoperability:** The ability of different IAM systems (e.g., on-prem AD and cloud Azure AD) to work together using standards like SAML, SCIM (for provisioning), and LDAP.
- **Attestation:** A periodic review where a manager or data owner confirms that a user's current access permissions are still appropriate. This is a maintenance activity to combat "permission creep."

## Section 4: Proving Identity – Authentication

**Multifactor Authentication (MFA)**

- **Definition:** Using two or more factors from different categories to authenticate.
- **Factors:**
    1. **Something you know:** Password, PIN.
    2. **Something you have:** Smart card, hardware token (YubiKey), phone (soft token app like Google Authenticator), security key.
    3. **Something you are:** Biometric (fingerprint, facial recognition).
    4. **Somewhere you are:** Geolocation/IP address (can be a weak factor).
- **Implementations:**
    - **Biometrics:** Convenient but raises privacy concerns; can have false acceptance/rejection rates.
    - **Hard/Soft Tokens:** Generate time-based one-time passwords (TOTP). Hard tokens are physical devices; soft tokens are apps.
    - **Security Keys (FIDO2/WebAuthn): Phishing-resistant.** The key uses public-key cryptography to prove identity. The future of MFA.

**Implementation Scenario:** To secure a remote access VPN, you would implement MFA, requiring a password (something you know) and a code from a mobile authenticator app (something you have).

**Password Concepts & Passwordless**

- **Password Best Practices:**
    - **Length > Complexity:** A long passphrase (CorrectHorseBatteryStaple) is stronger and more memorable than a short complex one (P@ssw0rd!).
    - **No Reuse:** Enforce via technical controls.

  - **Limit Expiration/Age:** NIST now recommends **not forcing regular password changes** unless there is evidence of compromise, as it leads to weak, predictable patterns.
- **Password Managers:** Tools that generate and store strong, unique passwords. Enhance security by promoting their use.
- **Passwordless Authentication:** Eliminates the password factor entirely. Uses something you have + something you are. Examples: Windows Hello (biometric + device), FIDO2 security keys.

## Section 5: The Crown Jewels – Privileged Access Management (PAM)

PAM is IAM for administrator and service accounts. These accounts are high-value targets.

**Privileged Access Management Tools**

- **Password Vaulting:** Stores privileged passwords in an encrypted vault. Admins **check out** a password to use it, and it's automatically rotated after use. Provides logging and breaks the "shared admin password" problem.
- **Just-in-Time (JIT) Permissions:** Elevated privileges are granted temporarily only when needed for a specific task, then automatically revoked. Reduces the standing attack surface.
- **Ephemeral Credentials:** Short-lived credentials generated for a single session or task, often used in cloud environments (AWS IAM roles).

**Implementation Scenario:** To control and monitor access to network routers, you would implement a PAM solution that requires admins to connect through a jump server, check out router credentials from a password vault, and have their session fully logged.

# Chapter Summary

Implementing and maintaining IAM is about enforcing policy through technology across the identity lifecycle:

1. **Onboard/Offboard** users cleanly (Provisioning/De-provisioning).
2. **Authenticate** strongly (MFA, Passwordless).
3. **Authorize** precisely (RBAC, ABAC, Least Privilege).
4. **Simplify** user experience (SSO via SAML/OIDC).
5. **Control** high-risk access (PAM with Vaulting & JIT).
6. **Maintain** through reviews (Attestation).

The goal is to ensure the right people have the right access to the right resources at the right time—and for the right reasons.

**Exam-Related Tips**

1. SAML = Enterprise Web SSO. OAuth = Delegated API Access. OIDC = Modern App Authentication.
2. RBAC = Groups/Roles. The answer for scalable permission management in a company.
3. Just-in-Time & Password Vaulting are for Privileged Access Management.
4. MFA Factors: Something you have = token/key. Something you are = biometric.
5. Password Best Practice: Length over complexity. Avoid frequent forced changes.
6. De-provisioning is critical to prevent orphaned accounts.

**Think Like the Exam**

*Scenario: "A company is migrating its on-premises email to a cloud service. Management wants employees to log into the cloud email portal using their existing Active Directory username and password, without having to create new credentials. Which of the following should be implemented to meet this requirement in a secure manner?"*

- Requirement: Use existing AD credentials for a cloud web application.
- This is a classic web SSO scenario between an on-prem directory (IdP) and a cloud app (SP).
- The secure, standard way to do this is to establish a federation trust using the SAML protocol.

- **Correct Answer:** Implement SAML-based SSO where the on-premises Active Directory is configured as the Identity Provider (IdP) for the cloud email service.

**Self-Reflection Prompt**

Look at the apps on your phone. How many use SSO (e.g., "Sign in with Apple" or "Sign in with Google")? That's OIDC. How many ask for a password and then a code from an app? That's MFA. For your most important account (like email), what access control model do you use? (You likely use DAC—you own your data and decide who to share it with). This connects everyday tech use to enterprise IAM concepts.

# Chapter 20 – The Force Multiplier: Automation & Orchestration

## Exam Objective 4.7: Explain the importance of automation and orchestration related to secure operations

*Chapter Introduction*

Imagine a security team of three people trying to manually manage 10,000 servers, respond to 500 alerts daily, and provision accounts for a company of 5,000. It's impossible. This is where automation and orchestration become your superpower. Automation is about replacing manual, repetitive tasks with scripts and tools. Orchestration is about coordinating multiple automated tasks into a seamless, intelligent workflow (like a digital conductor). This chapter explores how these concepts transform security from a reactive, human-limited function into a proactive, scalable, and resilient operation. For the Security+ exam, you need to understand the *why*—the compelling benefits—and the *how*—the specific use cases that make operations secure.

**Security+ Exam Mindset**

This objective is about justification and comprehension. CompTIA will ask you to identify the primary benefit of automation in a given scenario or to recognize a valid use case. You won't be writing scripts, but you must understand how automation solves efficiency/time-saving problems like scale, consistency, and speed. Be ready to weigh benefits against potential drawbacks.

## Section 1: The "What" – Key Use Cases

Automation is applied to the most repetitive, error-prone, and time-sensitive tasks in security ops.

**User & Resource Lifecycle Management**

- **User Provisioning/De-provisioning:** Automatically create, modify, or disable user accounts across all systems (AD, email, SaaS apps) based on triggers from an HR system. *This eliminates orphaned accounts and ensures timely access.*

- **Resource Provisioning:** Using Infrastructure as Code (IaC) tools (Terraform, CloudFormation) to automatically spin up pre-hardened, compliant servers and networks in the cloud. Every deployment is identical and follows the secure baseline.

**Policy Enforcement & Guard Rails**

- **Security Groups & Guard Rails:** In cloud environments, you can automate the enforcement of policies that prevent misconfigurations. Example: An automated script or cloud-native tool (like AWS Config) that immediately detects and reverts any S3 bucket set to public, acting as a safety guard rail.
- **Enabling/Disabling Services & Access:** Automatically disable network access for a device that fails a NAC health check, or disable a user's access at 5:05 PM based on time-of-day policy.

**Incident Response & Workflow**

- **Ticket Creation & Escalation:** When a SIEM generates a high-severity alert, automation can create a ticket in the IT service management (ITSM) system, assign it to the SOC, and even escalate it via SMS if not acknowledged in 15 minutes.
- **Initial Response Actions:** Orchestration platforms (SOAR) can execute a **pre-defined playbook**: isolate an infected endpoint (quarantine), block the malicious IP at the firewall, and snapshot the VM for forensic analysis—all within seconds of alert detection.

**Development & Integration (DevSecOps)**

- **Continuous Integration and Testing:** Automatically running SAST, SCA, and DAST tools every time a developer commits code. Security is "shifted left" into the development pipeline.
- **Integrations and APIs:** The glue that makes automation possible. Security tools expose APIs so that a SIEM can talk to a firewall, a ticketing system, and an endpoint tool, allowing for coordinated, automated responses.

## Section 2: The "Why" – Overwhelming Benefits

**Core Security Benefits**

- **Enforcing Baselines & Standard Configurations:** Automation guarantees consistency. Every system is built from the same hardened IaC template or configured by the same script. This eliminates configuration drift, the #1 cause of security gaps.

- **Scaling in a Secure Manner:** You can deploy 1 or 1000 servers with the same level of security assurance. Automation allows security to keep pace with business growth.
- **Improved Reaction Time:** Automated responses act at machine speed. Containing a malware outbreak in minutes instead of hours can mean the difference between a minor incident and a catastrophic breach.

**Operational & Human Benefits**

- **Efficiency/Time Saving:** Frees security analysts from mundane tasks (password resets, log review) to focus on complex threat hunting and analysis.
- **Workforce Multiplier:** A small team can manage a vast, complex environment effectively.
- **Employee Retention:** Reduces burnout from repetitive, tedious work and empowers analysts with more interesting, strategic tools.

## Section 3: The Reality Check – Other Considerations

Automation is powerful, but not a magic wand. It introduces new risks that must be managed.

**Other Considerations**

- **Complexity:** Automated systems and scripts can become incredibly complex, making them difficult to understand, troubleshoot, and audit.
- **Cost:** Initial investment in tools, training, and development time can be high. However, this is typically offset by long-term efficiency gains.
- **Single Point of Failure:** If your automation/orchestration platform is compromised, an attacker could trigger malicious actions at scale (e.g., disabling all firewalls). It must be **heavily secured and monitored**.
- **Technical Debt:** Poorly written, undocumented scripts become a liability. They break when systems change and nobody knows how to fix them.
- **Ongoing Supportability:** Automation requires maintenance. Scripts need updating as APIs change, new systems are added, and threats evolve. It's not "set and forget."

# Chapter Summary

Automation and orchestration are fundamental to modern, effective security operations. They directly enhance security by:

- **Making it consistent** (enforcing baselines).
- **Making it fast** (automated response).
- **Making it scalable** (managing cloud growth).

The key is to automate the right things—the repetitive, high-volume, well-defined tasks—while being acutely aware of the new risks automation introduces. The goal is to build a resilient, automated security layer that acts as a force multiplier for your human defenders, allowing them to focus their expertise where it's needed most.

**Exam-Related Tips**

1. IaC (Terraform, CloudFormation) = Automated, Consistent Resource Provisioning.
2. SOAR Platforms = Incident Response Orchestration (ticket creation, isolation, blocking).
3. Guard Rails are automated policy enforcement in the cloud (e.g., "no public S3 buckets").
4. The primary benefit is often Consistency, Speed, or Scalability. Match the benefit to the scenario.
5. A major risk is Single Point of Failure. If the question asks for a downside, this is a key one.
6. APIs are the enablers that allow tools to integrate and automate.

**Think Like the Exam**

*Scenario: "After several incidents involving misconfigured cloud storage buckets that were accidentally set to public, a company wants to ensure this cannot happen in the future. Which of the following automation use cases would BEST address this risk?"*

- The problem: Misconfiguration leading to data exposure.
- The goal: Prevent the misconfiguration from being possible or immediately correct it.
- The BEST automation use case is to implement Guard Rails. This would involve writing a script or using a cloud-native tool that continuously monitors for storage buckets with public access and automatically changes the configuration back to private, or better yet, prevents the 'public' setting from being selected at all through policy.

- This is more proactive than just alerting (which is detection, not prevention).

**Self-Reflection Prompt**

Think about your own digital routines. What's one security task you do manually that could be automated? (e.g., checking for software updates, reviewing privacy settings). What would be the benefit (time saved, less likely to forget)? What might be a drawback (if the automation breaks, you might miss something)? This applies the enterprise concept to personal security hygiene.

# Chapter 21 – When the Alarm Sounds: Incident Response Activities

## Exam Objective 4.8:

## Explain appropriate incident response activities

*Chapter Introduction*

The firewall failed. The phishing email was clicked. The zero-day was exploited. Now what? Incident response (IR) is the organized, methodical approach to handling a security breach or cyberattack. It's the difference between chaotic panic and controlled resolution. This chapter walks through the industry-standard Incident Response Lifecycle, detailing what you do in each phase—from preparing your team *before* an incident, to detecting and analyzing the threat, containing the damage, eradicating the attacker, recovering your systems, and learning from the event to improve. For the Security+ exam, you must know the order, purpose, and key activities of each phase, as well as related disciplines like forensics and threat hunting.

**Security+ Exam Mindset**

This is a sequential and procedural objective. CompTIA loves to test the order of the IR phases and ask scenario-based questions like, "After isolating an infected host, what is the NEXT step?" You must also understand the nuances between similar phases (Containment vs. Eradication) and the legal aspects of forensics. Think in terms of a structured process.

## Section 1: The Incident Response Lifecycle

This is the core framework. Memorize the order and goal of each phase.

**Response Lifecycle Steps**

*1. Preparation*

- **Goal:** Get ready *before* an incident occurs. This is the most critical phase.
- **Activities:**
    - Develop and document IR plans and policies.
    - Establish an IR team with clear roles (CISO, Lead, PR, Legal).
    - Assemble toolkits (forensic software, secure comms).
    - Conduct training and testing (tabletop exercises, simulations).

*2. Detection & Analysis*

- **Goal:** Determine if an incident is occurring and understand its scope and impact.
- **Activities:**
  - **Detection:** Identifying anomalies via monitoring (SIEM alerts, IDS, user reports).
  - **Analysis:** Triage to weed out false positives. Gather evidence (logs, memory dumps, network traffic). Determine the attack vector, scope, and impact. Classify the incident severity.

*3. Containment*

- **Goal:** Stop the bleeding. Prevent the incident from causing further damage.
- **Activities:** This has two sub-phases:
  - **Short-term Containment:** Immediate action to limit damage. Example: Disconnecting an infected machine from the network (quarantine), blocking a malicious IP at the firewall.
  - **Long-term Containment:** Applying temporary fixes to allow business to continue while eradication is planned. Example: Rebuilding a clean system for the user while the infected one is analyzed.

*4. Eradication*

- **Goal:** Remove the root cause of the incident from the environment.
- **Activities:** Find and eliminate all components of the threat. This includes:
  - Removing malware from infected systems.
  - Identifying and disabling attacker persistence mechanisms (backdoors, rogue accounts).
  - Patching the vulnerability that was exploited.

**Key Distinction: Containment isolates the threat; Eradication removes it.**

*5. Recovery*

- **Goal: Restore affected systems and operations** to normal, securely.
- **Activities:**
  - Carefully restore systems from clean backups.
  - **Reconnect systems** to the network.
  - **Monitor** closely for any signs of re-infection.

- Validate that systems are functioning correctly.

*6. Post-Incident Activity (Lessons Learned)*

- **Goal: Improve future security posture and response.**
- **Activities:**
  - Hold a "lessons learned" meeting with all involved stakeholders.
  - Complete a detailed incident report.
  - Update IR plans, policies, and procedures based on findings.
  - **Root Cause Analysis (RCA):** A formal process to determine the underlying, fundamental cause of the incident to prevent recurrence (e.g., "The breach occurred due to an unpatched server." RCA asks: "Why was it unpatched? Lack of patch management process?")**.

## Section 2: Readiness – Training & Testing

You don't wait for a real incident to practice.

### Training & Testing

- Training: Ensure the IR team and general staff know their roles. Staff should know how to report an incident.
- Tabletop Exercise: A discussion-based walkthrough of a hypothetical incident scenario. Cheap, effective for testing plans and communication.
- Simulation: A more realistic, hands-on drill that may involve simulated attacks on a test environment. Tests technical skills and tool usage.

## Section 3: Proactive & Investigative Activities

### Threat Hunting

- A proactive activity conducted *during peacetime* (or based on a hypothesis). It involves actively searching through networks and datasets to find adversaries that have evaded existing security controls. It's based on the assumption that a breach has already occurred.

### Digital Forensics

The application of scientific methods to collect, preserve, analyze, and present digital evidence in a way that is legally admissible. Digital forensics runs parallel to the IR process, especially during Analysis and Eradication.

- **Legal Hold:** A formal notification to preserve all relevant data (logs, emails, files) because it may be used in legal proceedings.
- **Chain of Custody:** A documented paper trail that records who handled evidence, when, why, and what changes were made. Critical for evidence integrity in court.
- **Acquisition:** The process of collecting evidence in a forensically sound manner (e.g., creating a bit-for-bit copy/image of a hard drive, not working on the original).
- **Preservation:** Protecting the original evidence from alteration. This includes storing media in a secure, access-controlled location.
- **E-Discovery (Electronic Discovery):** The process of identifying, collecting, and producing electronically stored information (ESI) in response to a legal request or investigation.
- **Reporting:** Documenting all forensic findings in a clear, concise report for management, legal teams, or law enforcement.

# Chapter Summary

An effective incident response is a disciplined, phased approach:

1. **PREPARE** (Plan, Train, Tool up).
2. **DETECT & ANALYZE** (Confirm, Scope, Triage).
3. **CONTAIN** (Isolate to prevent spread).
4. **ERADICATE** (Find and remove root cause).
5. **RECOVER** (Restore operations securely).
6. **LEARN** (Improve via lessons learned and RCA).

Throughout, forensic principles (chain of custody, preservation) must be followed if legal action is possible. Threat hunting is the proactive cousin of IR, searching for hidden threats before they cause a major incident. The ultimate goal is to minimize damage, recovery time, and costs.

**Exam-Related Tips**

1. **Order is Sacred:** Preparation -> Detection/Analysis -> Containment -> Eradication -> Recovery -> Lessons Learned. Containment comes BEFORE Eradication.
2. **Containment = Isolate/Quarantine.** Eradication = Remove malware/patch.
3. **Chain of Custody** is for **legal admissibility** of evidence.
4. **Tabletop Exercise = Discussion-based test.** Simulation = Hands-on test.
5. **Root Cause Analysis (RCA)** happens in the Lessons Learned phase to prevent recurrence.
6. **Threat Hunting is Proactive,** based on the assumption you're already breached.

**Think Like the Exam**

*Scenario: "A SOC analyst confirms that a workstation is infected with ransomware that is encrypting files on a network share. The analyst's first action is to disconnect the workstation from the network. According to the incident response process, which phase does this action belong to, and what should be the NEXT phase?"*

- The action of disconnecting the workstation is Short-term Containment (stopping the spread).
- According to the lifecycle, after Containment comes Eradication.

- **Correct Answer:** The action is part of the Containment phase. The next phase is Eradication, where the analyst would remove the ransomware from the workstation, identify how it got in, and patch that vulnerability.

**Self-Reflection Prompt**

Think of a non-cyber "incident" like a flat tire. Map your response to the IR phases: Preparation (having a spare and jack), Detection (hearing the thump, seeing the low pressure), Analysis (pulling over, assessing damage), Containment (putting on the donut spare to get off the highway), Eradication (getting the tire repaired/replaced), Recovery (putting the good tire back on), Lessons Learned ("I should avoid that pothole-filled road"). This analogy makes the structured process intuitive.

# Chapter 22 – Following the Evidence: Data Sources for Investigation

## Exam Objective 4.9:

## Given a scenario, use data sources to support an investigation

*Chapter Introduction*

Every incident leaves a trail. Your job as a security investigator is to be a digital detective, following that trail through the vast amounts of data your systems generate. This chapter is your guide to the evidence locker—the logs, captures, and reports that tell the story of what happened. You'll learn *where* to look for specific clues and *how* different data sources complement each other to build a complete picture. For the Security+ exam, you must be able to match an investigative question (e.g., "How did the attacker get in?" or "What data was exfiltrated?") with the most likely data source that holds the answer.

**Security+ Exam Mindset**

This is a practical, matching objective. CompTIA will give you a specific investigative goal and a list of data sources. You must choose the best one or the first one you'd check. Focus on the unique value of each data source: what does it tell you that others don't? Think like an investigator piecing together a timeline.

## Section 1: The Primary Evidence – Log Data

Logs are the chronicles of your digital environment. Each type answers different questions.

**Firewall Logs**

- What they tell you: Network connection attempts—source/destination IP, port, protocol, and whether traffic was allowed or denied.
- **Investigative Use:**
  - **"How did they get in?"** Look for allowed inbound connections to exploited services.
  - **"Where did they go?"** Look for suspicious outbound connections from compromised hosts to external C2 servers.

   - **“What did they try to access?”** Look for repeated denied attempts (brute force, scanning).

**Application & Web Server Logs**

- What they tell you: User interactions with an application—HTTP requests, URLs accessed, form inputs, errors.
- **Investigative Use:**
   - **Web Attack Investigation:** Look for patterns of SQL injection (strings with ‘ OR ‘1’=‘1) or XSS (strings with <script>) in URL parameters or form fields.
   - **Account Compromise:** Look for failed login attempts followed by a successful login from a different IP.

**Endpoint Logs (Windows Event Logs / Linux Syslog)**

- **What they tell you: Activity on a specific computer.**
   - **Windows Security Logs:** Authentication events (Successful/Failed logons, logon type), account management (user created), process creation.
   - **Linux Syslog/auditd:** Similar events: user logins, sudo commands, and file accesses.
- **Investigative Use:**
   - **“What did the attacker do on the host?”** Look for unusual process execution, scheduled task creation, or registry modifications.
   - **“Which user account was compromised?”** Correlate malicious activity with a specific logon session.

**Operating System-Specific Security Logs**

- This includes the detailed audit logs mentioned above. They are critical for understanding local actions on a system.

**IPS/IDS Logs**

- **What they tell you:** Alerts and events related to detected attack patterns or anomalies.
- **Investigative Use:** Provides a curated list of suspicious activity based on signatures or behavior. A good starting point to understand the *type* of attack (e.g., “IDS alerted on a buffer overflow attempt against the FTP server”).

**Network Logs (NetFlow, sFlow, IPFIX)**

- **What they tell you:** Metadata about network conversations—"who talked to whom, when, and how much." Not the content, just the headers.
- **Investigative Use:**
    - **Data Exfiltration:** Identify large, sustained outbound data transfers to an unknown external IP.
    - **Lateral Movement:** Spot unusual internal connections (e.g., HR workstation connecting to a database server).
    - **DDoS Detection:** See massive inbound traffic flows from many sources.

**Metadata**

- **What it is:** Data about data. File metadata includes creation date, author, edit history. Email metadata includes sender, recipient, timestamps, routing path.
- **Investigative Use:** Establishing timelines and provenance. "When was this malicious file created?" "Did this email really come from the claimed sender?"

## Section 2: Supporting Intelligence – Other Data Sources

**Vulnerability Scan Reports**

- **What they tell you:** A point-in-time assessment of known weaknesses on systems.
- **Investigative Use:** After an incident, consult recent scans. Was the exploited vulnerability present and known? This can reveal failures in the patch management process. It answers "Could this have been prevented?"

**Automated Reports & Dashboards**

- **What they tell you:** Summarized, high-level trends (e.g., "Top 10 attacking IPs this week," "Patch compliance status").
- **Investigative Use:** Provide context and prioritization. A dashboard showing a spike in malware alerts from a specific department can point you where to start digging.

**Packet Captures (PCAP)**

- **What they tell you:** The full, raw contents of network traffic. The ultimate source of truth for what was transmitted.
- **Investigative Use:**
    - **Deep Analysis:** Reconstruct malicious files transferred, extract credentials sent in clear-text, or reverse-engineer a custom C2 protocol.

  - **Validation:** Confirm hypotheses formed from log data (e.g., "The firewall log shows an allowed connection on port 443; the PCAP shows it was actually an SSH tunnel disguised as HTTPS.").
- **Important:** PCAPs are large and may contain sensitive data. Their use is often governed by privacy policies.

# Chapter Summary

A successful investigation relies on correlating multiple data sources to build a timeline and understand the scope.

- To understand NETWORK activity: Start with Firewall and NetFlow logs.
- To understand HOST activity: Dive into Endpoint and OS Security logs.
- To understand APPLICATION attacks: Analyze Application and Web Server logs.
- To get the FULL CONTENT of communications: Use Packet Captures (PCAP).
- To understand the CONTEXT of weaknesses: Review Vulnerability Scan reports.

The investigator's skill is in knowing which log to pull first to answer the specific question at hand and then following the clues across different sources to get the full story.

**Exam-Related Tips**

1. **"How did they get in?" = Firewall Logs** (look for allowed inbound) or **IDS Logs** (look for exploit alert).
2. **"What did they take?" = NetFlow Logs** (look for large outbound transfers) or **Endpoint Logs** (look for file access).
3. **"What did they do on the host?" = Endpoint/OS Security Logs** (process creation, account events).
4. **SQLi/XSS investigation = Web Server/Application Logs.**
5. **Packet Captures (PCAP) = Ultimate detail,** used for deep analysis and confirmation.
6. **Vulnerability Scans = Pre-incident context,** to see if the hole was known.

**Think Like the Exam**

*Scenario: "An investigator suspects that a compromised internal workstation is being used to exfiltrate sensitive research documents to an external server. The data is likely being transferred over HTTPS. Which data source would be MOST useful in confirming the data transfer and estimating the volume of data involved?"*

- The data is going out over HTTPS (encrypted).
- A Packet Capture (PCAP) would show the encrypted traffic but not the contents, and would be very large to analyze just for volume.

- Firewall logs would show the connection but not indicate the amount of data transferred.
- NetFlow logs are perfect for this. They provide metadata showing a sustained, high-volume flow from the internal workstation IP to an external IP on port 443 (HTTPS), which would strongly indicate data exfiltration and show exactly how much data was sent.
- **Correct Answer:** Network Logs (NetFlow).

**Self-Reflection Prompt**

Think of a recent time you had to troubleshoot a tech problem (e.g., website not loading, app crashing). What "logs" or "data sources" did you check? (e.g., error message on screen = application log; internet connectivity = network log). This is the same investigative mindset—you start with the most relevant source of information for the symptom you're seeing.

# Domain 5: Security Program Management and Oversight

# Chapter 23 – The Rulebook: Elements of Effective Security Governance

## Exam Objective 5.1:

## Summarize elements of effective security governance

*Chapter Introduction*

Security isn't just a technical problem; it's a management and governance problem. You can have the best firewall in the world, but if there's no policy telling employees how to create strong passwords, it's useless. Security governance is the framework of rules, roles, and responsibilities that guides an organization's overall security strategy and ensures it aligns with business goals. This chapter covers the hierarchy of governance documents (policies, standards, procedures), the external forces that shape them (laws, regulations), and the people accountable for making it all work. For the Security+ exam, you must understand the *purpose* and *relationship* between these elements and who is ultimately responsible for security decisions.

**Security+ Exam Mindset**

This objective tests your knowledge of security frameworks and hierarchy. You'll need to distinguish between a policy, a standard, and a procedure. You'll also need to know the purpose of common policies (like AUP) and understand how external regulations drive internal governance. Expect definitional questions and scenario-based questions about accountability (e.g., "Who is responsible for classifying data?").

## Section 1: The Governance Hierarchy – Policies, Standards, Procedures

Think of this as a pyramid from broad goals to specific steps.

**Policies, Standards, Procedures**

**1. Policies (The "What" and "Why")**

- **Definition:** High-level, strategic documents approved by senior management that state the organization's security goals, principles, and overall stance. They are mandatory.

- **Purpose:** To inform the entire organization of management's security expectations. They are the foundation.
- **Key Policies:**
    - **Acceptable Use Policy (AUP):** Defines the acceptable ways employees can use company IT resources (email, internet, computers). What is and isn't allowed.
    - **Information Security Policy:** The overarching policy that defines the purpose, scope, and objectives of the security program.
    - **Business Continuity (BC) & Disaster Recovery (DR) Policy:** Defines the commitment to maintaining operations during and after a disruption.
    - **Incident Response (IR) Policy:** Authorizes the creation of an IR team and plan, and defines management's support for it.
    - **Software Development Lifecycle (SDLC) Policy:** Mandates that security be integrated into all phases of software development.
    - **Change Management Policy:** Requires that all changes follow a formal process to minimize risk.

**2. Standards (The "How" – Specific Rules)**

- **Definition:** Mandatory, detailed rules that support a policy. They define *specific* technologies, configurations, or actions required to meet the policy's goals.
- **Purpose:** Ensure uniformity and security baselines across the organization.
- **Key Standards:**
    - **Password Standard:** Specifies minimum length (e.g., 12 characters), complexity, expiration (if any), and history.
    - **Access Control Standard:** Defines the use of RBAC, least privilege, and regular access reviews.
    - **Physical Security Standard:** Specifies requirements for badges, locks, visitor logs, and surveillance.
    - **Encryption Standard:** Mandates the use of specific algorithms (AES-256) and key lengths for data at rest and in transit.

**3. Procedures (The "Step-by-Step Instructions")**

- **Definition:** Detailed, sequential instructions for personnel to follow to accomplish a specific security task or comply with a standard/policy.

- **Purpose:** Ensure tasks are performed consistently and correctly.
- **Key Procedures:**
  - **Change Management Procedure:** The exact steps for submitting, approving, testing, and implementing a change.
  - **Onboarding/Offboarding Procedure:** Checklists for provisioning/de-provisioning user accounts and equipment.
  - **Incident Response Playbooks:** Step-by-step guides for handling specific types of incidents (e.g., "Ransomware Playbook").

**Relationship:** A **Policy** states you must have strong passwords. A Standard defines what "strong" means (12 chars, complexity). A Procedure shows an admin how to set those requirements in Active Directory.

## Section 2: External Forces – The "Must-Do" List

Governance isn't created in a vacuum; it's heavily influenced by external requirements.

**The "Must-Do" List**

- **Regulatory/Legal:** Laws you must obey (e.g., HIPAA for healthcare in the US, GDPR for data privacy in the EU). Non-compliance results in fines and legal action.
- **Industry:** Standards you may **choose** to follow to demonstrate security (e.g., ISO 27001, PCI DSS for handling credit cards). Often required by partners or customers.
- **Local/Regional/National/Global:** The jurisdiction matters. Data stored in Germany is subject to German law. A global company must navigate a complex web of these requirements.

**Impact:** External considerations directly shape your internal policies. A GDPR compliance requirement will lead to a Data Privacy Policy and Data Retention Procedures.

## Section 3: Keeping It Alive – Monitoring & Revision

**Monitoring & Revision**

- Governance is not static. Policies must be reviewed and updated regularly (e.g., annually) or when significant changes occur (new regulations, major incident).
- Monitoring ensures the policies are being followed (through audits, scans, and reviews).

## Section 4: Who's in Charge? – Governance Structures & Roles

### Governance Structures

- **Boards & Committees:** Senior groups (like a Security Steering Committee) that provide oversight, approve policies, allocate budget, and prioritize security initiatives. They link security to business strategy.
- **Government Entities:** For public sector organizations.
- **Centralized vs. Decentralized:**
    - **Centralized:** Security governance is controlled by a single, central team (e.g., corporate CISO). Ensures consistency.
    - **Decentralized:** Business units have significant control over their own security. Can be faster but risks inconsistency.

### Critical Roles & Responsibilities (Especially for Data)

- **Data/System Owner:** A senior business executive (e.g., VP of Sales) who is ultimately accountable for a specific data set or system. They determine its classification, approve access, and bear the business risk. *The Buck Stops Here.*
- **Data Controller (GDPR term):** The entity that determines the purposes and means of processing personal data. This is typically the organization itself.
- **Data Processor:** An entity that processes data on behalf of the Controller (e.g., a cloud payroll provider). Bound by contract.
- **Data Custodian/Steward:** The IT or security personnel tasked with implementing the owner's directives. They handle the day-to-day security controls (backups, access provisioning, encryption). They are *responsible for* security, but the Owner is *accountable*.

# Chapter Summary

Effective security governance provides the authority, direction, and clarity needed for a successful security program.

- It's built on a hierarchy: Policies (goals) -> Standards (rules) -> Procedures (steps).
- It is shaped by external regulations (GDPR, HIPAA) and industry standards (PCI DSS).
- It is overseen by committees and executed by people with clear roles, most importantly the Data Owner (accountable) and Data Custodian (responsible).
- It is a living framework that must be monitored and revised.

Without governance, security is just a collection of technical controls without strategic purpose or clear accountability.

**Exam-Related Tips**

1. Policy = Management's Mandate. Standard = Specific Technical Rule. Procedure = Step-by-Step Instructions.
2. AUP = Acceptable Use of Company IT.
3. Data Owner = Business Executive, Accountable. Data Custodian = IT Staff, Responsible.
4. GDPR = Key Regulation for Data Privacy (Controllers & Processors).
5. Governance must be reviewed and updated regularly.

**Think Like the Exam**

*Scenario: "The legal department informs the CISO that a new state law requires all customer data to be encrypted both at rest and in transit. The CISO needs to ensure IT systems comply. Which of the following governance elements should the CISO create or update FIRST to formally address this new legal requirement?"*

- A new legal requirement has been introduced.
- To ensure organization-wide compliance, you need a mandatory rule that aligns with the business's strategic goal of obeying the law.
- The FIRST step is to update or create a high-level Policy (e.g., the Information Security Policy or a Data Protection Policy) that states the organization's commitment to encrypting customer data as required by law.

- This policy would then drive the creation or update of an Encryption Standard (to specify *how* to encrypt) and Procedures (to implement it).

**Self-Reflection Prompt**

Think of a club or team you've been part of. What were its "policies" (e.g., "Members must attend meetings")? Its "standards" (e.g., "Members must wear the team shirt to games")? Its "procedures" (e.g., "Step 1: Collect dues. Step 2: Log payment.")? Who was the "owner" accountable for the team's success? This analogy makes corporate governance relatable.

# Chapter 24 – Playing the Odds: The Risk Management Process

## Exam Objective 5.2:
## Explain elements of the risk management process

*Chapter Introduction*

Cybersecurity isn't about achieving "perfect security" (impossible). It's about managing risk intelligently. Risk is the potential for loss or damage when a threat exploits a vulnerability. The risk management process is the systematic way an organization identifies, analyzes, and decides what to do about its risks. This chapter walks you through that entire process: from finding risks (identification) and measuring them (assessment/analysis), and making the critical business decision on how to handle them (strategies). For the Security+ exam, you must understand the workflow, the key formulas (SLE, ALE, ARO), and the crucial business concepts of tolerance and appetite. This is where security meets the boardroom.

**Security+ Exam Mindset**

This objective is conceptual and quantitative. CompTIA will ask you to define stages of the process, differentiate between qualitative and quantitative analysis, and apply the risk formulas in simple scenarios. You'll also need to match a described business stance (e.g., "we never take risks") to the correct risk strategy. Focus on understanding the *purpose* of each element and how they connect.

## Section 1: Finding the Risks – Identification & Assessment

**Risk Identification**

- **What it is:** The process of finding, recognizing, and describing risks that could affect the organization.
- **How it's done:** Through methods like threat modeling, vulnerability scans, audits, and brainstorming sessions. The goal is to create a comprehensive list of potential risks.

**Risk Assessment & Analysis (Often used together)**

- **Risk Assessment:** The overall process of identifying, analyzing, and evaluating risk. It can be:
-

- **Ad hoc:** Done for a specific project or event.
- **Recurring:** Done on a regular schedule (e.g., annually).
- **One-time:** For a specific purpose.
- **Continuous:** Using automated tools to constantly monitor for new risks (ideal).

- **Risk Analysis:** The step within assessment where you *measure* the identified risks.

**Risk Analysis Methods**

- **Qualitative Analysis:** Uses scales and categories (e.g., High/Medium/Low) based on expert opinion and experience. Faster, subjective, easier to communicate.
  - *Example:* "The risk of phishing is High Likelihood and Medium Impact."
- **Quantitative Analysis:** Uses numerical values and data (dollars, percentages). More objective but requires more data.
  - **Key Formulas:**
    - **Single Loss Expectancy (SLE):** The cost of a single occurrence of a risk. SLE = Asset Value (AV) × Exposure Factor (EF)
      - *Example:* A server (AV=$10,000) damaged by fire with an EF of 30% (partial loss) has an SLE of $3,000.
    - **Annualized Rate of Occurrence (ARO):** The estimated number of times a risk is expected to occur in a year.
      - *Example:* You expect a fire in your data center once every 20 years → ARO = 0.05.
    - **Annualized Loss Expectancy (ALE):** The expected monetary loss per year for a given risk. ALE = SLE × ARO
      - *Example:* SLE ($3,000) × ARO (0.05) = ALE of **$150 per year**.
  - **Why it matters:** ALE helps you decide if a control is cost-effective. If a $5,000 firewall reduces the ALE of an outage from $10,000 to $1,000 (saves $9,000), it's a good investment.

## Section 2: Documenting & Deciding – The Risk Register & Business Stance

**Risk Register**

- **What it is:** The master document (often a spreadsheet or database) that tracks all identified risks, their analysis, and their treatment status.
- **Key Elements in a Register:**
    - **Risk Owners:** The person accountable for managing that specific risk.
    - **Key Risk Indicators (KRIs):** Metrics that warn when a risk is increasing (e.g., "number of unpatched critical servers" is a KRI for exploitation risk).
    - **Risk Threshold:** The specific level of risk that, if exceeded, triggers an action or escalation.

**Risk Appetite vs. Risk Tolerance**

- **Risk Appetite:** The total amount and type of risk an organization is willing to pursue or accept to achieve its objectives. It's a high-level, strategic statement.
    - **Expansionary:** Willing to take on significant risk for high growth (common in startups).
    - **Conservative:** Seeks to minimize risk (common in banks, utilities).
    - **Neutral:** Somewhere in between.
- **Risk Tolerance:** The acceptable deviation from the risk appetite for a specific objective or process. It's more operational and measurable.
    - *Analogy:* Appetite is "I'm willing to drive on highways." Tolerance is "I will not exceed 75 mph."

## Section 3: Taking Action – Risk Management Strategies

Once a risk is analyzed, you must decide what to do about it. There are four core strategies:

**Risk Management Strategies**

1. **Accept:** Acknowledge the risk and take no action. Done when the cost of mitigation exceeds the potential loss (ALE is low) or the risk aligns with the organization's appetite. This is a conscious business decision, not negligence.

  - **Exception/Exemption:** A formal, documented approval to accept a risk for a limited time or under specific conditions (e.g., "We accept the risk of not patching this legacy system for 60 days while a replacement is built.").

2. **Mitigate (Treat):** Take steps to reduce the likelihood or impact of the risk. This is what most security controls do (firewalls, patches, training).
3. **Transfer:** Shift the financial burden of the risk to a third party. The primary method is cybersecurity insurance. Outsourcing to a cloud provider also transfers some operational risk.
4. **Avoid:** Eliminate the risk entirely by stopping the activity that causes it. Example: Deciding not to launch a new, risky online service.

## Section 4: Planning for Impact – Business Impact Analysis (BIA)

The BIA is a **subset of risk management** focused on understanding the effects of a disruption and planning for recovery.

**Business Impact Analysis (BIA)**

- **Recovery Time Objective (RTO):** The maximum acceptable downtime for a system or process. "How long can we be down?" Determines if you need a hot, warm, or cold site.
- **Recovery Point Objective (RPO):** The maximum acceptable data loss measured in time. "How much data can we afford to lose?" Determines backup frequency.
- **Mean Time to Repair (MTTR):** The average time it takes to fix a failed component and restore service. A measure of your repair capability.
- **Mean Time Between Failures (MTBF):** The average time a system or component operates before it fails. A measure of reliability.

**Risk Reporting**

- Communicating risk information (from the risk register, assessments, BIA) to stakeholders (management, board, auditors) to support informed decision-making.

# Chapter Summary

Risk management is the core decision-making engine of security. It's a continuous cycle:

1. IDENTIFY what could go wrong.
2. ANALYZE it (Qualitatively or Quantitatively using SLE, ARO, ALE).
3. DOCUMENT it in a Risk Register with an owner and KRIs.
4. EVALUATE it against the organization's Risk Appetite and Tolerance.
5. TREAT it using a strategy: Mitigate, Transfer, Avoid, or Accept.
6. PLAN for impact using BIA concepts (RTO, RPO).
7. REPORT and MONITOR.

The goal is not to eliminate all risk, but to make informed, cost-effective decisions that align security with business objectives.

**Exam-Related Tips**

1. SLE = AV × EF. ALE = SLE × ARO. Be able to do simple math with these.
2. Qualitative = High/Medium/Low. Quantitative = Dollar amounts.
3. Risk Acceptance is a formal, documented decision, not doing nothing.
4. Risk Appetite = Strategic willingness. Risk Tolerance = Operational limit.
5. RTO = Time to restore. RPO = Data loss tolerance.
6. Risk Transfer = Insurance.

**Think Like the Exam**

*Scenario: "A company estimates that a successful phishing attack against its finance department would result in a direct financial loss of $50,000 (SLE). Historical data suggests such an attack is likely to occur twice a year (ARO). The company is considering a new security awareness training program that costs $15,000 per year and is expected to cut the number of successful attacks in half. What is the ALE before and after the training, and is the training cost-justified?"*

1. **ALE before training:** SLE ($50,000) × ARO (2) = $100,000
2. **ALE after training:** New ARO = 1 (half of 2). SLE ($50,000) × ARO (1) = $50,000
3. **Annual Savings:** $100,000 - $50,000 = $50,000
4. **Cost of Control:** $15,000

5. **Justification:** The training saves $50,000 per year and costs $15,000. It is highly cost-effective.

**Self-Reflection Prompt**

Think of a personal risk you manage, like car ownership. Go through the process: Identify (risk of an accident), Analyze (cost of repair, likelihood based on your driving), Evaluate (your personal risk tolerance—do you have a deductible you can afford?), Treat (you mitigate by driving safely, and transfer by buying insurance). This makes the corporate process feel personal and logical.

# Chapter 25 – Your Weakest Link: Managing Third-Party Risk

## Exam Objective 5.3:
## Explain the processes associated with third-party risk assessment and management

*Chapter Introduction*

Your company's security is only as strong as the *weakest link in your supply chain.* A breach at a cloud provider, a software vendor, or even the cleaning company with after-hours access can still become *your company's* breach. Third-party risk management (TPRM) is the process of identifying, assessing, and controlling the risks posed by external organizations that have access to your data, systems, or facilities. This chapter covers the full lifecycle: how to vet a vendor before you sign, what to put in the contract, and how to monitor them after. For the Security+ exam, you must understand that risk isn't just internal and that specific legal and assessment tools are used to manage external relationships.

**Security+ Exam Mindset**

This objective is about **processes and documentation**. CompTIA will ask you to identify the correct step in the vendor lifecycle (assessment, selection, agreement, monitoring) or to match a security requirement with the specific document that enforces it (e.g., SLA, MOU, NDA). Focus on the *purpose* of each agreement type and the *tools* used for assessment.

## Section 1: The Investigation – Vendor Assessment

Before you do business, you must investigate their security.

**Vendor Assessment Methods**

- **Penetration Testing:** You (or a firm you hire) may conduct a pen test on the vendor's systems (with their permission) to identify vulnerabilities they might have missed.
- **Right-to-Audit Clause:** A critical contractual provision that gives you the legal right to audit the vendor's security controls and compliance periodically. Without this, you're trusting their word.

- **Evidence of Internal Audits:** Requesting copies of the vendor's own internal audit reports or compliance certifications (e.g., SOC 2 Type II report, ISO 27001 certification). This is less intrusive than your own audit.
- **Independent Assessments:** Relying on audits performed by reputable third parties (like the **SOC 2** report from a CPA firm). This is a standard and efficient way to gain assurance.
- **Supply Chain Analysis:** Investigating not just your direct vendor, but their vendors (your 4th party risk). For example, if your SaaS provider uses a subcontracted data center, you need to know the security of that data center.

**Questionnaires**

- A standard tool for initial assessment. You send the vendor a detailed security questionnaire (often based on frameworks like SIG, CAIQ) to self-report on their security practices. Useful for screening, but must be verified.

## Section 2: Making the Choice – Vendor Selection

**Due Diligence**

- The comprehensive process of investigating a vendor's financial health, reputation, and security posture before entering into a contract. The assessment activities above are part of due diligence.
- **Purpose:** To avoid partnering with a risky vendor that could fail or cause a security incident.

**Conflict of Interest**

- Ensuring that the vendor selection process is fair and unbiased. For example, a decision-maker should not have a financial stake in the vendor being selected. This is an ethical and governance requirement.

## Section 3: The Rulebook – Agreement Types

The contract is where you formalize security expectations and obligations. Each document type serves a specific purpose.

**Agreement Types**

- **Service-Level Agreement (SLA):** The most technical and measurable agreement. It defines the specific performance standards the vendor must meet, often with penalties (service credits) for failure.

  - *Example:* "Email service must have 99.9% uptime. If it drops below, we receive a 10% service credit."

- **Memorandum of Understanding (MOU) / Memorandum of Agreement (MOA):** Less formal than a contract. An MOU is a statement of mutual intent to cooperate (a "handshake" in writing). An MOA is slightly more formal, outlining specific cooperative responsibilities. Often used between government agencies or in early partnership stages.
- **Master Service Agreement (MSA):** The overarching contract that sets the standard terms and conditions for all future work between two parties. Individual projects are then defined under the MSA using...
- **Work Order (WO) / Statement of Work (SOW):** Defines the specific scope, deliverables, and timeline for a particular project or service engagement. The "what" and "when" of a specific task.
- **Non-Disclosure Agreement (NDA):** A confidentiality agreement. Legally binds both parties to not disclose each other's sensitive information shared during the relationship.
- **Business Partners Agreement (BPA):** A broad agreement that governs an ongoing strategic partnership, often covering IP, revenue sharing, and mutual commitments beyond a simple buyer-seller relationship.

## Section 4: Keeping Watch – Vendor Monitoring

Risk management doesn't stop at the contract signing.

**Vendor Monitoring**

- **Continuous Monitoring:** You must periodically reassess the vendor's security. This can involve:
  - Reviewing their annual SOC 2 report.
  - Monitoring news for breaches or incidents involving the vendor.
  - Exercising your Right-to-Audit clause if red flags appear.
- **Rules of Engagement:** A documented set of rules governing how security testing (like penetration testing) will be conducted against the vendor's systems. It defines scope, timing, methods, and communication protocols to ensure testing is authorized and safe.

# Chapter Summary

Third-party risk management is a continuous, four-phase lifecycle:

1. **ASSESS:** Investigate the vendor's security using questionnaires, audits (SOC 2), and **penetration testing**. Secure a Right-to-Audit clause.
2. **SELECT:** Choose a vendor after due diligence, avoiding conflicts of interest.
3. **AGREE:** Formalize the relationship with the right documents:
    - **SLA** for performance metrics.
    - **MSA/SOW** for project terms.
    - **NDA** for confidentiality.
4. **MONITOR:** Continuously oversee the vendor's performance and security posture, using reports and audits.

The core principle: You cannot outsource responsibility. If your vendor has a breach that exposes your data, it's still *your* breach in the eyes of customers and regulators. Therefore, you must actively manage the risk they introduce.

**Exam-Related Tips**

1. Right-to-Audit Clause = Your legal right to check their security. A must-have.
2. SOC 2 Report = Independent audit report you should request from a cloud/SaaS vendor.
3. SLA = Specific, measurable uptime/performance metrics with penalties.
4. MSA = Overall contract. SOW = Specific project details.
5. NDA = Confidentiality agreement.
6. Due Diligence is the research you do BEFORE selection.

**Think Like the Exam**

*Scenario: "A company is contracting with a new Software-as-a-Service (SaaS) provider that will host sensitive customer data. The company's legal team is concerned about ensuring the provider maintains a strong security posture and wants the ability to verify it periodically. Which of the following should be a REQUIRED clause in the contract to address this concern?"*

- The requirement is for ongoing, verifiable assurance of the vendor's security.
- Requesting an initial report (like SOC 2) is good, but it's a point-in-time check.
- The need is for the ability to verify periodically.

- The Right-to-Audit clause is specifically designed for this. It grants the customer the contractual right to assess the vendor's controls, either themselves or through a third party, at defined intervals or under specific conditions.
- **Correct Answer: Right-to-Audit clause.**

**Self-Reflection Prompt**

Think of a service you use that holds your personal data (e.g., a cloud storage provider). You are the "company," and they are the "vendor." What questions (questionnaire) would you want to ask them about their security? What agreement (SLA) would you care about? (e.g., uptime, data breach notification). This applies TPRM concepts to your personal digital life.

# Chapter 26 – Playing by the Rules: Effective Security Compliance

## Exam Objective 5.4:
## Summarize elements of effective security compliance

*Chapter Introduction*

Compliance is the concrete proof that your security program isn't just good on paper—it meets real-world rules. These rules come from laws, regulations, industry standards, and even your own contracts. Effective compliance isn't about checking boxes to avoid punishment; it is about building a systematic program to understand requirements, implement controls, prove you're following them, and continuously monitor for gaps. This chapter ties together governance, risk, and operations within the compliance function. For the Security+ exam, you need to grasp the full compliance lifecycle, the severe consequences of failure, and the critical privacy principles that dominate modern regulations.

**Security+ Exam Mindset**

This objective is about understanding programmatic elements and consequences of non-compliance. CompTIA will ask about the *components* of a compliance program (reporting, monitoring) and the *results* of non-compliance. You'll also need to understand key privacy terminology (controller, processor, right to be forgotten) which is central to regulations like GDPR. Focus on the "why" behind each activity.

## Section 1: Proving It – Compliance Reporting

Reporting is how you demonstrate compliance to stakeholders.

**Compliance Reporting**

- **Internal Reporting:** Providing compliance status to management and the board. Examples include dashboards showing patch compliance percentages and reports on open audit findings. Purpose: Informs business decisions and oversight.
- **External Reporting:** Providing evidence to outside entities. This includes:
  - **Regulators:** Submitting required documentation to agencies like the SEC, HHS (for HIPAA), or EU data protection authorities.
  - **Auditors:** Furnishing evidence for SOC 2, ISO 27001, or PCI DSS audits.

  - **Customers/Partners:** Responding to security questionnaires as part of their vendor risk assessment.

**Key Point:** Effective reporting relies on accurate, auditable evidence gathered from your security controls and monitoring activities.

## Section 2: The Stakes – Consequences of Non-Compliance

Failing to comply is not an abstract concept; it has tangible, severe consequences.

**Consequences**

- **Fines and Sanctions:** Direct financial penalties. GDPR fines can be up to 4% of global annual revenue. HIPAA violations can reach $1.5 million per year. These are game-changers for businesses.
- **Reputational Damage:** Loss of customer and partner trust after a publicized violation. This can be more damaging than fines in the long term.
- **Loss of License:** For highly regulated industries (finance, healthcare), non-compliance can result in the **revocation of the license to operate**.
- **Contractual Impacts:** Breach of contract with customers or partners, leading to **termination of agreements, lawsuits, and financial liabilities**.

**Why it Matters:** These consequences make compliance a core business risk, not just an IT issue. They justify investment in the compliance program.

## Section 3: The Continuous Cycle – Compliance Monitoring

Compliance is not a one-time audit. It requires ongoing vigilance.

**Compliance Monitoring**

- **Due Diligence/Care:** The legal concept of taking reasonable steps to comply with laws and protect data. It's the foundation of your monitoring efforts—showing that compliance was actively maintained.
- **Attestation and Acknowledgement:** Attestation is a formal verification (often by an executive) that controls are in place and effective. Acknowledgement is having employees formally confirm they've read and agree to follow policies (like the AUP).
- **Internal vs. External Monitoring:**
  - **Internal:** Your own team conducts audits, scans, and reviews to find and fix gaps *before* an external audit. This is often referred to as self-policing.

- **External:** Independent third-party audits (like a PCI QSA or a firm performing a SOC 2 audit) provide objective validation that builds trust.

- **Automation:** Using tools to continuously check configurations against baselines (SCAP), monitor for policy violations, and generate evidence. This turns compliance from a painful, manual annual event into a real-time, manageable process.

## Section 4: The Modern Imperative – Privacy

Data privacy has become the centerpiece of global compliance, driven largely by the EU's GDPR and similar laws.

**Privacy**

- **Legal Implications:** Laws exist at all levels:
  - **Local/Regional:** US state laws (California's CCPA/CPRA, Virginia's VCDPA).
  - **National:** Country-specific laws (Brazil's LGPD, Canada's PIPEDA).
  - **Global:** GDPR applies to any organization that process personal data of EU citizens, regardless of where the organization is located.
- **Key Privacy Roles (GDPR Specific):**
  - **Data Subject:** The individual whose personal data is being processed (the customer, employee, website visitor).
  - **Data Controller:** The organization that determines the purposes and means of processing personal data (you, the company).
  - **Data Processor:** An organization that processes data on behalf of the Controller (e.g., your cloud provider, payroll service). The Controller is responsible for the Processor's actions.
- **Ownership:** A critical concept. While the organization *controls* the data, the Data Subject has rights over their own personal data. This is a fundamental shift from pure ownership.
- **Data Inventory and Retention:** To comply, you must know what data you have, where it is, why you have it, and how long you keep it. A data inventory is mandatory. Retention policies must be enforced to delete data when it's no longer needed for its original purpose.
- **Right to be Forgotten (Erasure):** A powerful GDPR right. A Data Subject can request that the Controller erase their personal data under specific conditions (e.g., withdrawal of consent). You must have a process to locate and delete all instances of that person's data.

# Chapter Summary

Effective security compliance is an active, evidence-based management program that integrates with your overall security operations.

1. It requires clear reporting (internal and external) to demonstrate adherence.
2. It is motivated by serious consequences (fines, reputational harm) for failure.
3. It is sustained through continuous monitoring, combining internal checks, external audits, and automation.
4. In today's world, it is dominated by data privacy regulations (GDPR, CCPA) which emphasize the rights of the Data Subject, the responsibilities of Controllers and Processors, and principles like data minimization and the right to be forgotten.

Ultimately, a strong compliance program turns regulatory requirements into operational habits, making security more consistent, defensible, and trustworthy.

**Exam-Related Tips**

1. GDPR = Fines up to 4% of global revenue. A key consequence.
2. Controller vs. Processor: The Controller calls the shots and is ultimately liable. The Processor acts on the Controller's instructions.
3. Right to be Forgotten = Data Erasure upon request.
4. Compliance Monitoring requires both Internal and External activities.
5. Automation is key for continuous compliance (e.g., SCAP scans).
6. Data Inventory is a foundational step for privacy compliance.

**Think Like the Exam**

*Scenario: "A multinational company receives a request from a former customer in France to have all their personal data permanently deleted from the company's systems. Under which regulation is this right primarily granted, and which role within the company is ultimately responsible for ensuring the request is fulfilled?"*

- The request is for data erasure from a person in France (EU).
- The right to erasure is a core tenet of the GDPR.
- The company that collected and decides how to use the data is the Data Controller.

- **Correct Answer:** The right is granted under the GDPR, and the Data Controller is responsible for ensuring the request is fulfilled (even if the actual deletion work is done by a Processor).

**Self-Reflection Prompt**

Think about an app or website you've used that asked for your consent to use cookies or collect data. That's a direct result of privacy compliance (GDPR/CCPA). Imagine you wanted to exercise your "right to be forgotten" with that company. What steps would you expect them to have in place? This connects the abstract regulation to your real-world digital interactions.

# Chapter 27 – The Check-Up: Types and Purposes of Audits & Assessments

## Exam Objective 5.5:

## Explain types and purposes of audits and assessments

*Chapter Introduction*

You've built your security program, implemented controls, and managed risks. But how do you *know* it's actually working? That's where audits and assessments come in—they're the check-ups and stress tests for your security health. This chapter breaks down the different flavors: from internal self-checks to high-stakes external exams, and from compliance checklists to simulated attacks (penetration tests). For the Security+ exam, you need to understand who conducts each type, their purpose, and key concepts like the "attestation" that gives them weight.

**Security+ Exam Mindset**

This objective is about categorization and intent. CompTIA will ask you to differentiate between an internal audit and an external audit, or to identify the type of penetration test based on the tester's knowledge. Focus on the *goal* of each activity: Is it for compliance? For finding technical flaws? For proving security to outsiders?

## Section 1: The Official Stamp – Attestation

**Attestation**

- **Attestation:** A formal, written declaration and verification (often by an independent third party) that specific security controls are in place and operating effectively.
- **Purpose:** Provides assurance and trust to stakeholders (management, board, customers, regulators). It's the documented *proof* that your controls work.
- **Common Form:** The SOC 2 (System and Organization Controls) report is a classic attestation report from a CPA firm. It doesn't just list controls; it *attests* to their design and operating effectiveness.

## Section 2: Looking Inward – Internal Audits & Assessments

Conducted by or for the organization itself, for its own benefit.

**Internal Audits & Assessments**

- **Internal Compliance Audits:** Performed to ensure the organization is following its own policies, standards, and procedures. Checks for adherence to internal governance.
- **Audit Committee:** A sub-group of the Board of Directors responsible for overseeing internal and external audits, financial reporting, and compliance. They ensure audit independence and receive findings.
- **Self-Assessments:** A less formal process where departments or process owners evaluate their own controls against a framework (e.g., using a checklist). Prone to bias but useful for continuous improvement.

**Purpose of Internal Activities:** Proactive gap identification and improvement. To find and fix problems before an external auditor or attacker does.

## Section 3: Outside Verification – External Audits & Assessments

Conducted by **independent parties outside the organization**.

**External Audits & Assessments**

- **Regulatory Examinations:** Conducted by government agencies to enforce laws. Examples: A HIPAA audit by the Office for Civil Rights (OCR), a bank examination by the FDIC. These activities are high-stakes and mandatory.
- **Independent Third-Party Audit:** Hired by the organization but performed by an independent, accredited firm (e.g., a PCI QSA for PCI DSS, a CPA firm for SOC 2). Provides credible, objective assurance to external parties.
- **Assessment:** A broader term that can be less formal than an audit. Could be a vulnerability assessment (technical scan) or a risk assessment (evaluating threats/vulns).

**Purpose of External Activities:** To provide objective verification for compliance, build customer trust, and meet contractual or legal obligations.

## Section 4: The Attack Simulation – Penetration Testing

A specialized, authorized, simulated attack to evaluate security by exploiting vulnerabilities. It’s an assessment with a specific methodology.

**Perspectives & Integration**

- **Physical Penetration Test:** Attempting to gain physical access to buildings, servers, or sensitive areas (e.g., tailgating, lock picking).
- **Offensive vs. Defensive:**
    - **Offensive Security (Red Team):** The attackers. Their goal is to breach defenses, often with stealth and persistence, mimicking a real adversary.
    - **Defensive Security (Blue Team):** The defenders. Their goal is to detect, respond to, and thwart the Red Team's attacks.
- **Integrated (Purple Teaming):** Red and Blue Teams work together collaboratively in real-time to improve detection and response capabilities. The goal is learning and improvement, not just scoring.

**Tester Knowledge & Scope (The "Box" Metaphor)**

- **Known Environment (White Box):** The tester has full knowledge of the internal system (network diagrams, source code). Goal: A deep, thorough assessment of specific systems that is efficient.
- **Partially Known Environment (Gray Box):** The tester has some knowledge (e.g., user-level credentials, system architecture). Mimics an insider threat or an attacker with initial access. Balanced approach.
- **Unknown Environment (Black Box):** The tester has no prior knowledge, just a target name (like a public company name). Mimics an external attacker with no inside info. Tests perimeter defenses and public footprint.

**Reconnaissance Phase**

The first phase of any penetration test or attack: *information gathering.*

- **Passive Reconnaissance:** Gathering information without interacting directly with the target. Generally cannot be detected.
    - *Methods:* Searching public records (OSINT), using Google dorking, reviewing social media, analyzing DNS records.
- **Active Reconnaissance:** Directly interacting with the target to learn more. Can be detected.
    - *Methods:* Port scanning (Nmap), vulnerability scanning, pinging hosts.

# Chapter Summary

Audits and assessments are the verification layer of security management. They answer the critical question: "Are we doing what we say we're doing, and does it work?"

- Internal audits are for self-improvement and preparing for external scrutiny.
- External audits/assessments provide independent validation for compliance and trust.
- Penetration tests are controlled attacks that measure technical resilience, varying based on tester knowledge (White/Gray/Black Box) and starting with reconnaissance (Passive/Active).

Together, they form a feedback loop that drives the continuous maturity of your security program, moving from theory to proven practice.

**Exam-Related Tips**

1. SOC 2 Report = Independent Third-Party Attestation.
2. Internal Audit = For self-improvement. External Audit = For compliance/trust.
3. White Box = Full knowledge. Black Box = No knowledge. Gray Box = Some knowledge.
4. Passive Recon = Undetectable (OSINT). Active Recon = Scans, can be detected.
5. Physical Pen Test = Testing physical security controls (doors, badges).
6. Purple Teaming = Red + Blue collaborating.

**Think Like the Exam**

*Scenario: "A financial services company is required by regulation to undergo an annual security review. The review must be performed by a certified, independent party and must test both technical controls and organizational processes. The results will be submitted to a government regulator. Which type of activity is being described?"*

- Required by **regulation**.
- Performed by an **independent, certified party**.
- Tests both technical and process controls.
- Results go to a **government regulator**.
- This describes a Regulatory Examination or an Independent Third-Party Audit mandated by regulation. It's more formal than a generic assessment and has direct legal consequences.

**Self-Reflection Prompt**

Think of a time you prepared for a big test or inspection (e.g., a car inspection, a final exam). You likely did a self-assessment (practice tests, checking your car's lights) first. That's your internal audit. The official test/inspection is the external audit. This analogy highlights the purpose of checking your own work before the high-stakes review.

# Chapter 28 – The Human Firewall: Implementing Security Awareness

## Exam Objective 5.6:

## Given a scenario, implement security awareness practices

*Chapter Introduction*

The most advanced firewall in the world can't stop an employee from clicking a malicious link. Technology secures systems, but people secure organization. Security awareness is about turning your workforce from the weakest link into the strongest defense—the "human firewall." This final operational chapter focuses on the practical programs and training initiatives that empower employees to recognize threats, follow policies, and protect data. For the Security+ exam, you need to know how to structure an effective awareness program, from running phishing simulations to teaching hybrid work security.

**Security+ Exam Mindset**

This is a practical, programmatic objective. CompTIA will give you a scenario about a security weakness stemming from human behavior (e.g., "Employees are falling for spear-phishing" or "USB drives are being lost") and ask you to select the appropriate awareness practice to address the weakness. Focus on matching the training topic to the specific risk.

### Section 1: The #1 Threat – Phishing Awareness

Phishing is the primary initial attack vector. Your awareness program must tackle it head-on.

**Phishing Campaigns (Simulations)**

- **What it is:** Sending simulated phishing emails to employees to test their vigilance in a safe environment.
- **Purpose:** Measurable training. It identifies which employees are susceptible, provides immediate feedback when they "fail," and raises overall awareness. Data from campaigns guides further training.
- **Implementation:** Start with obvious phishing attempts and gradually increase sophistication. Never punish employees for failing—use it as a teachable moment.

**Recognizing a Phishing Attempt**

Training must cover the telltale signs:

- Urgent or threatening language ("Your account will be closed!").
- Generic greetings ("Dear Valued Customer").
- Suspicious sender addresses (support@amaz0n-security.com).
- Mismatched links (hover to see the real URL).
- Requests for sensitive information or unexpected attachments.

**Responding to Reported Suspicious Messages**

- Establish a clear, easy reporting process (e.g., a "Report Phish" button in Outlook).
- Train users to report, not delete. Reported emails become intelligence for the security team to analyze and potentially block threats for the entire organization.
- Provide positive reinforcement when users report successfully.

## Section 2: Beyond Phishing – Anomalous Behavior Recognition

Teach employees to trust their instincts about "weird" activity.

**Behavior Recognition**

- **Risky Behavior:** Actions that knowingly increase risk (e.g., using unauthorized cloud storage for work files, disabling security software for "performance").
- **Unexpected Behavior:** Unusual activity that could indicate a compromise (e.g., a coworker accessing files at 3 AM, a computer running unusually slow, strange pop-ups).
- **Unintentional Behavior:** Mistakes that happen to everyone (e.g., accidentally emailing a sensitive document to the wrong person, misplacing a USB drive).
- **Training Focus:** Employees should know how to report anomalous behavior (risky, unexpected, or unintentional) through the proper channels without fear of undue blame.

## Section 3: Core Training Topics – User Guidance

A comprehensive program covers these essential areas.

**User Guidance**

- **Policy/Handbook Review:** Ensure employees read and acknowledge key policies (Acceptable Use Policy, Data Handling Policy). This is the foundation of awareness.
- **Situational Awareness:** Being mindful of one's surroundings. **In the office:** noting tailgaters at secure doors. **In public:** shoulder surfing at coffee shops.

- **Insider Threat Awareness:** Helping employees understand that insider threats can be malicious OR negligent, and teaching them the signs of a potentially malicious insider (e.g., disgruntled behavior, attempts to access unauthorized data).
- **Password Management:** Training on creating strong passphrases, using password managers, and never reusing passwords across work and personal accounts.
- **Removable Media and Cables:** Dangers of unknown USB drives (USB baiting attacks), the importance of encrypting portable drives, and risks of juice jacking via public charging ports/cables.
- **Social Engineering:** Expanding beyond phishing to include vishing (phone scams), smishing (SMS), and pretexting (fabricated scenarios). Teach the common tactics: authority, urgency, scarcity.
- **Operational Security (OPSEC):** The discipline of protecting sensitive information about organizational activities. For example, not discussing confidential projects on social media or in public places.
- **Hybrid/Remote Work Environments:** Specialized training for risks outside the office:
    - Securing home Wi-Fi (WPA3, strong password).
    - **Locking screens** when stepping away.
    - Proper **document disposal** (shredding, not home trash).
    - Risks of mixing personal and work activities on the same device.

## Section 4: Building the Program – Development, Execution, Reporting

### Development

- Identify needed training based on a risk assessment (what are our biggest human risks?) and past incidents.
- Tailor content to different roles (e.g., finance needs more BEC training, developers need secure coding).
- Use engaging formats (short videos, interactive modules, gamification) for Gen Z/Millennial learners.

### Execution

- Initial Training: For all new hires as part of onboarding. Non-negotiable.
- Recurring Training: Annual mandatory training for all employees, with shorter, topical refreshers (e.g., quarterly 5-minute videos) to keep awareness high.

**Reporting and Monitoring**

- Track metrics to measure program effectiveness:
    - Phishing click-through rates (are they going down?).
    - Number of incidents reported by users, which should increase as awareness improves.
    - Training completion rates.
- Report these metrics to management to demonstrate ROI and justify the program.
- Use monitoring to identify repeat offenders or high-risk departments for targeted, additional training.

# Chapter Summary

Implementing security awareness is about creating a culture of shared responsibility. It's a continuous cycle:

1. **DEVELOP** engaging training based on your organization's specific risks (phishing, data handling, remote work).
2. **EXECUTE** through mandatory initial and recurring sessions, using simulations (phishing campaigns) for hands-on learning.
3. **TRAIN** on core topics: recognizing anomalous behavior, password hygiene, social engineering, and hybrid work risks.
4. **REPORT AND MONITOR** metrics to demonstrate value and improve the program.

The goal is to make secure behavior automatic and intuitive for every employee, transforming them from a target into an active defender.

**Exam-Related Tips**

1. Phishing Campaigns = Simulated emails for training and measurement.
2. "Report, Don't Delete" is the mantra for suspicious messages.
3. Initial Training = Onboarding. Recurring Training = Annual + refreshers.
4. Hybrid/Remote Training must cover home Wi-Fi security and screen locking.
5. Metrics (like phishing click rate) are used to report on the program's effectiveness to management.
6. USB Baiting/Juice Jacking are key physical/digital hybrid threats to cover.

**Think Like the Exam**

*Scenario: "A company has seen an increase in lost corporate USB drives, some containing unencrypted sensitive data. The security team wants to address this human risk through the awareness program. Which TWO training topics would be MOST effective in mitigating this specific risk?"*

- The risk: Lost removable media with sensitive data.
- To mitigate, you need to address both the physical loss and the data exposure.
    1. **Training on Removable Media:** Policies against using unencrypted USB drives, and procedures for using approved, encrypted drives.

2. **Data Handling/Classification Training:** So employees understand what data is "sensitive" and therefore should never be placed on an unencrypted portable device in the first place.

- Topics like phishing or passwords, while important, don't directly address this specific scenario.

**Self-Reflection Prompt**

Think about the last time you received a suspicious email or text. Did you recognize it? What tipped you off? Now, imagine you're responsible for training your friends or family on that one tip. What would you say? That's the core of security awareness—breaking down complex threats into simple, actionable behaviors that people can remember and use.

# Bibliography

This eBook/textbook was developed using the official CompTIA Security+ (SY0-701) exam objectives and industry-standard cybersecurity frameworks. The following sources were referenced to ensure accuracy, alignment with exam requirements, and real-world applicability:*

**Primary Source & Certification Authority**

1. **CompTIA Security+ (SY0-701) Exam Objectives** (2023). CompTIA, Inc.

   *The definitive source for all exam topics, terminology, and structure referenced throughout this guide.*

**Official CompTIA Resources**

2. **CompTIA Security+ Certification Exam Objectives (SY0-701)**. CompTIA.

   *Official exam outline detailing domains, objectives, and sub-objectives.*

3. **CompTIA Security+ Certification Study Materials**. CompTIA.

   *Supplementary guidance on exam structure and recommended preparation.*

**Cybersecurity Frameworks & Standards**

4. **NIST Cybersecurity Framework (CSF) 2.0** (2024). National Institute of Standards and Technology.

   *Referenced for risk management, incident response, and security governance concepts.*

5. **NIST Special Publication 800-53** (Rev. 5). National Institute of Standards and Technology.

   *Security and privacy controls referenced for technical implementations.*

6. **NIST Special Publication 800-61** (Rev. 2). National Institute of Standards and Technology.

   *Computer Security Incident Handling Guide referenced for incident response procedures.*

7. **ISO/IEC 27001:2022**. International Organization for Standardization.

   *Information security management system (ISMS) standards referenced for governance.*

8. **CIS Critical Security Controls (CIS Controls) v8**. Center for Internet Security.

   *Practical security actions referenced for hardening and mitigation techniques.*

9. **MITRE ATT&CK Framework**. The MITRE Corporation.

   *Tactics, techniques, and procedures referenced for threat actor behaviors and detection.*

**Regulatory & Compliance References**

10. **General Data Protection Regulation (GDPR)**. European Union.

    *Referenced for privacy, data protection, and compliance requirements.*

11. **Health Insurance Portability and Accountability Act (HIPAA)**. U.S. Department of Health & Human Services.

    *Referenced for regulated data and healthcare security considerations.*

12. **Payment Card Industry Data Security Standard (PCI DSS) v4.0**. PCI Security Standards Council.

    *Referenced for payment card security and compliance requirements.*

**Technical Standards & References**

13. **OWASP Top Ten 2021**. Open Web Application Security Project.

    *Referenced for web application security vulnerabilities and mitigations.*

14. **CIS Benchmarks**. Center for Internet Security.

    *Secure configuration guidelines referenced for hardening baselines.*

15. **RFC Documents**. Internet Engineering Task Force (IETF).

    *Technical standards for protocols (TLS, IPsec, DNSSEC, etc.) referenced throughout.*

16. **CVSS v3.1 Specification**. Forum of Incident Response and Security Teams (FIRST).

    *Common Vulnerability Scoring System referenced for vulnerability management.*

**Industry Best Practices & Guides**

17. **Cloud Security Alliance (CSA) Security Guidance**. Cloud Security Alliance.

    *Referenced for cloud security concepts and shared responsibility model.*

18. **SANS Institute Security Awareness Resources**. SANS Institute.

    *Referenced for security awareness program development and phishing training concepts.*

19. **Zero Trust Architecture**. NIST Special Publication 800-207.

    *Referenced for Zero Trust principles and implementation concepts.*

**Supplementary Educational Resources**

20. **Cybersecurity & Infrastructure Security Agency (CISA) Resources**. CISA.

    *Alerts, advisories, and best practices referenced for current threat landscape.*

21. **National Initiative for Cybersecurity Education (NICE) Framework**. NIST.

    *Referenced for cybersecurity workforce roles and competency alignment.*

**Style & Pedagogical References**

22. **Plain Language Guidelines**. PlainLanguage.gov.

*Applied for clear, accessible explanation of complex technical concepts.*

23. **Generation Z Learning Preferences Research** (Various Studies, 2020-2023).

*Informed the scenario-driven, conversational, and visually-oriented instructional approach.*

**Note on AI Assistance**

This eBook/textbook was developed with the assistance of **DeepSeek AI** (by Deep Seek), **ChatGPT** and **Gemini** for content generation, organization, and explanatory text development. All technical content was rigorously verified against the primary sources listed above to ensure exam accuracy and real-world validity. The AI served as an instructional design and writing assistant under human direction and expert review.

**Recommended Further Reading**

For students seeking additional depth on specific topics:

- CompTIA Security+ Certification Official Study Guide (SY0-701)
- NIST Cybersecurity Framework Documentation
- OWASP Web Security Testing Guide
- Cloud Security Alliance Cloud Controls Matrix
- SANS Reading Room Whitepapers

**---:< End of Part I >:---**

# Part II – AI-Enhanced Learning & Prompts for AI-Enhanced Learning & Visualization

Part II transforms learning from passive reading into active creation.

This section includes carefully designed AI prompts that guide learners to:

- Summarize topics in their own words
- Generate practice questions and explanations
- Create custom learning activities
- Design infographics for complex security concepts
- Visualize architectures, threats, and controls

These prompts are optional but highly recommended for deeper mastery.

# Preface

**Welcome to the Future of Learning**

Artificial Intelligence isn't here to replace your knowledge—it's here to multiply it. With the right approach, AI becomes your personal study partner: generating unlimited examples, quizzes, metaphors, and practice scenarios tailored to your pace.

## Appendix A: Using AI as a Security+ Study Accelerator

**This appendix shows you how to strategically use AI tools (such as ChatGPT, Gemini, and Claude) to accelerate your mastery of CompTIA Security+.**

**How to Use This Toolkit**

The *AI-First Approach* transforms a generic chatbot into a smart, cybersecurity-focused tutor. By crafting purposeful prompts, you take control of the learning experience, not the AI.

The Golden Rules of AI Study

Before you begin, follow these essential guidelines:

1 **Trust but Verify**

AI can occasionally "hallucinate." Always validate exam-critical facts (e.g., port numbers, NIST guidelines, regulatory frameworks) using your official Security+ materials.

2 **Protect Private Data**

Never paste the following:

- Real personal or organizational data (PII)
- Passwords or credentials
- Proprietary scripts or network layouts

3 **Iterate for Clarity**

If the first response isn't right, adjust:

- "Explain that more simply."
- "Add more technical examples."
- "Rewrite as bullet points."

You are the director—the AI follows your commands.

Concept Mastery Prompts

Use these when you're stuck on a topic or want a clearer explanation.

◆ **To Simplify Complex Topics (ELI5)**

*"Explain [Zero Trust Architecture] as if I am 12. Use a castle or bank analogy."*

◆ **To Compare Confusing Terms**

*"Create a comparison table between [Symmetric Encryption] and [Asymmetric Encryption] including: Speed, Key Usage, Complexity, Common Use Cases."*

◆ **To Memorize Acronyms**

*"Create a funny mnemonic to help me remember the Cyber Kill Chain steps."*

AI can turn tricky concepts into stories you won't forget.

The "Virtual Lab" Simulation

Hands-on learning—without a physical lab setup. Practice thinking like a security professional.

▶ **Social Engineering Drill**

*"Play the role of a cautious employee. I will attempt a vishing attack. Correct me when I fail, and respond realistically."*

▶ **Log Analysis Practice**

*"Generate a sample Linux authentication log showing brute-force attempts. Then walk me through identifying the attack."*

▶ **Incident Response Tabletop Exercise**

*"Scenario: HR server hit by ransomware. Provide the first inject and ask my first step according to the IR lifecycle."*

You learn better **by doing**—even in simulation.

Exam Prep & Quizzing

Turn AI into your personalized exam generator.

📌 **Practice Questions**

*"Create five multiple-choice Security+ questions for Domain 3.2 (Cloud Security). Match CompTIA difficulty. Allow me to answer before revealing explanations."*

📌 **Flashcard Creation**

*"Generate 10 key Risk Management terms formatted as CSV (Term, Definition) for Anki/Quizlet import."*

📌 **Scenario-Based Questions**

*"Give me a Security+ performance-based scenario involving IAM misconfigurations and ask me what to do first."*

You can create endless study material—instantly.

Troubleshooting Your Prompts

If you're not getting useful output—assign the AI a role.

👨‍🏫 **Professor Persona**

*"Act as 'Professor Ifti,' a strict but supportive cybersecurity expert. Evaluate my answer and point out any inaccurate logic."*

🕵️‍♂️ **Red Team Persona**

*"Act as an ethical hacker evaluating my network. Suggest three likely attack paths an adversary might attempt."*

Personas sharpen focus and raise the difficulty—perfect for exam readiness.

Final Tip

The goal isn't to rely on AI—it's to *transform your understanding* through AI-powered reinforcement.

Master the prompts… and you master the exam.

# CompTIA Security+ SY0-701 AI Learning Prompts (Objectives 1.1 – 5.6)

**For Professor Ifti's Students**

Use these prompts with any AI assistant to accelerate your learning.

---

## DOMAIN 1 — General Security Concepts

---

### 1.1 Fundamental Security Concepts

**Prompt:**

*"Explain Confidentiality, Integrity, and Availability with real-world examples. Then create a scenario where all three are required and ask me follow-up questions to test my understanding."*

**Prompt:**

*"Teach me Zero Trust in simple terms. Include Control Plane vs. Data Plane, adaptive identity, PEP, policy engine, and implicit trust zones. Then quiz me with 10 questions."*

**Prompt:**

*"Describe honeypots, honeynets, honeyfiles, and honeytokens. Create a mini-case study where I must choose the best deception technology."*

**Prompt:**

*"Explain all physical security controls (bollards, vestibules, sensors, fencing, cameras). Provide pictures or diagrams if possible and ask me to identify what each one protects against."*

### 1.2 Change Management

**Prompt:**

*"Explain the entire change management process using a simple 'before and after' example. Include approval, testing, impact analysis, maintenance windows, and backout plans. Then give me a scenario to analyze."*

### 1.3 Cryptographic Solutions

**Prompt:**

*"Teach me PKI, certificates, encryption types, hashing, salting, and digital signatures. Use graphics and step-by-step flow diagrams. Then generate 15 Security+ exam-style questions."*

**1.4 Cryptographic Attacks**

**Prompt:**

*"Explain downgrade attacks, birthday attacks, collisions, and crypto misuse with examples. Ask me to identify weaknesses in sample network designs."*

# DOMAIN 2 — Threats, Vulnerabilities, and Mitigations

**2.1 Threat Actors & Motivations**

**Prompt:**

*"Compare nation-state attackers, insiders, hacktivists, organized crime, and unskilled attackers. Create four scenarios and ask me to identify the actor and motivation."*

**2.2 Attack Vectors & Surfaces**

**Prompt:**

*"List all attack vectors (email, SMS, USB, supply chain, wireless, social engineering). Then give me a 'spot the attack vector' exercise based on five different situations."*

**2.3 Vulnerabilities**

**Prompt:**

*"Explain OS, application, cloud, web, and mobile vulnerabilities. Show me a real-world vulnerability chain from exploit → impact."*

**2.4 Indicators of Malicious Activity**

**Prompt:**

*"Simulate a malicious attack and provide logs. Ask me to interpret indicators such as lockouts, login anomalies, resource consumption, impossible travel, and missing logs."*

**2.5 Mitigation Techniques**

**Prompt:**

*"Teach me segmentation, least privilege, hardening, patching, ACLs, encryption, and configuration enforcement. Then give me an enterprise environment and ask me to design a mitigation plan."*

# DOMAIN 3 — Security Architecture

## 3.1 Architecture & Infrastructure Models

**Prompt:**

*"Explain cloud vs. on-prem vs. hybrid, IaC, microservices, virtualization, SDN, containers, and IoT. Create a visual diagram for each and quiz me on where each model is most secure."*

## 3.2 Securing Enterprise Infrastructure

**Prompt:**

*"Walk me through how to secure an enterprise network step-by-step: zones, DMZ, WAF, jump servers, IPS/IDS, port security, VPNs, and SASE. Then evaluate the flaws in three network diagrams that you generate."*

## 3.3 Protecting Data

**Prompt:**

*"Explain data classifications, states of data, data sovereignty, geolocation, tokenization, masking, encryption, hashing. Give me real examples and test me with a classification scenario."*

## 3.4 Resilience & Recovery

**Prompt:**

*"Explain high availability, clustering, load balancing, failover, UPS, generators, COOP, backups, RTO/RPO. Create a DR plan for a hospital or university."*

# DOMAIN 4 — Security Operations

### 4.1 Secure Baselines & Hardening

**Prompt:**

*"Walk me through securing a workstation, server, router, switch, cloud VM, mobile device, and IoT device using baselines. Then give me a system to harden and ask me to document my steps."*

### 4.2 Asset Management

**Prompt:**

*"Explain asset identification, inventory, tracking, classification, and disposal. Create a scenario where improper asset management leads to a breach."*

### 4.3 Vulnerability Management

**Prompt:**

*"Simulate a vulnerability scan result. Ask me to identify false positives, prioritize findings, and write a remediation plan."*

### 4.4 Security Monitoring

**Prompt:**

*"Explain SIEM, logs, alerts, tuning, SNMP, NetFlow, DLP, antivirus, and endpoint monitoring. Then create sample logs and ask me what action should be taken."*

### 4.5 Enhancing Security with Controls

**Prompt:**

*"Give me examples of firewall rules, IDS signatures, URL filtering, email security, DMARC, DKIM, SPF, DNS filtering. Then test me by asking which control to implement in specific incidents."*

### 4.6 Identity & Access Management

**Prompt:**

*"Teach me all IAM concepts: provisioning, SSO, federation, RBAC, ABAC, MAC, least privilege, MFA factors, password policies, PAM, JIT access. Then create 10 IAM scenarios for me to solve."*

### 4.7 Automation & Orchestration

**Prompt:**

*"Explain SOAR, scripts, API integrations, automated ticketing, auto-scaling, security guardrails. Then ask me to design a workflow that uses automation to fix a security problem."*

### 4.8 Incident Response

**Prompt:**

*"Simulate a full incident response scenario including logs, indicators, containment steps, eradication tasks, and lessons learned. Evaluate my decisions."*

### 4.9 Investigation & Data Sources

**Prompt:**

*"Provide logs from IDS, firewall, OS, servers, SIEM dashboards, PCAP samples. Ask me to investigate and provide findings."*

# DOMAIN 5 — Security Program Management and Oversight

### 5.1 Governance

**Prompt:**

*"Teach me policies, standards, guidelines, procedures, governance structures, and regulatory frameworks. Then give me a company and ask me to design a full governance package."*

### 5.2 Risk Management

**Prompt:**

*"Explain SLE, ALE, ARO, qualitative vs. quantitative analysis, risk register, risk scoring. Then give me five risks and ask me to calculate the ALE and recommend mitigation strategies."*

### 5.3 Third-Party Risk

**Prompt:**

*"Create a vendor risk assessment checklist based on SLA, MSA, MOA, NDA, audits, and right-to-audit clauses. Then evaluate a risky vendor scenario."*

### 5.4 Compliance

**Prompt:**

*"Explain compliance reporting, fines, sanctions, legal implications, privacy, data retention, and right to be forgotten. Ask me exam-style scenario questions."*

### 5.5 Audits & Assessments

**Prompt:**

*"Explain internal vs. external audits, penetration testing types, ROE, active vs. passive reconnaissance. Create a penetration test scenario for me to solve."*

### 5.6 Security Awareness

**Prompt:**

*"Simulate a phishing campaign and ask me to identify red flags. Then teach me insider threats, password hygiene, removable media risks, and social engineering defense."*

# CompTIA Security+ SYO-701 — Hands-On AI Lab Prompts (Objectives 1.1 – 5.6)

***(Copy/paste into ChatGPT, Gemini, or Copilot)***

---

## DOMAIN 1 — General Security Concepts (Labs)

---

### 1.1 CIA, Zero Trust, Physical Security, Deception Labs

**◆ Lab: CIA Triad Attack Simulation**

**Prompt:**

*"Simulate a small company suffering three different attacks: a confidentiality breach, an integrity attack, and an availability disruption. Walk me through detection, impact, and mitigation. Then give me 5 questions to confirm I understand how CIA applies."*

**◆ Lab: Zero Trust Network Access (ZTNA) Simulation**

**Prompt:**

*"Act as a Zero Trust controller. Ask me who is requesting access, what resource they want, device health, and risk context. Then decide whether to allow or deny access and explain why. Include Policy Engine and PEP decisions."*

**◆ Lab: Physical Security Walkthrough**

**Prompt:**

*"Create a virtual building with bollards, fencing, guard stations, cameras, vestibules, sensors, and badge readers. Let me move through the building and try to enter the data center while you challenge me at every step."*

**◆ Lab: Deploying Deception Tech**

**Prompt:**

*"Set up a fake internal network with honeypots, honeyfiles, and honeytokens. Let me place the deception tools, then run a simulated attacker and show me which traps they trigger."*

● **1.2 Change Management Labs**

◆ **Lab: Full Change Request Simulation**

**Prompt:**

*"Guide me through a complete change management cycle: request, approvals, testing, impact analysis, maintenance window, implementation, verification, and backout planning. Include surprises or conflicts during the process."*

● **1.3 Cryptography Labs**

◆ **Lab: PKI Certificate Lifecycle Simulation**

**Prompt:**

*"Simulate a full PKI environment. Allow me to generate CSRs, issue certificates, revoke them, check OCSP/CRL, and troubleshoot a TLS handshake failure caused by certificate misconfigurations."*

◆ **Lab: Encryption in Practice**

**Prompt:**

*"Give me sample plaintext data. Then let me choose whether to encrypt it with symmetric, asymmetric, or hashing. Show me how to decrypt or validate it. Include errors if I choose the wrong method."*

● **1.4 Cryptographic Attack Labs**

◆ **Lab: Cracking Weak Hashes**

**Prompt:**

*"Simulate an attacker attempting a birthday attack or a collision attack. Allow me to strengthen the hashing process with salting, stretching, and updated algorithms. Show before/after effects."*

## DOMAIN 2 — Threats, Vulnerabilities, Mitigations (Labs)

### 2.1 Threat Actors

**◆ Lab: Identify the Threat Actor**

**Prompt:**

*"Give me four cyber incidents. In each case, hide the threat actor identity but include subtle clues. Ask me to identify whether it's nation-state, insider, hacktivist, or cybercriminal and explain my reasoning."*

### 2.2 Threat Vectors

**◆ Lab: Attack Vector Hunt**

**Prompt:**

*"Create a network with email, SMS, IoT devices, BYOD, outdated software, default creds, and social engineering vulnerabilities. Ask me to locate all attack vectors and propose mitigations."*

### 2.3 Vulnerabilities

**◆ Lab: Vulnerability Mapping**

**Prompt:**

*"Present me with logs, web pages, APIs, cloud misconfigurations, and mobile device issues. Ask me to identify vulnerabilities such as SQLi, buffer overflows, VM escape, and cryptographic misconfigurations."*

### 2.4 Malicious Activity Indicators

**◆ Lab: Analyze Malicious Logs**

**Prompt:**

*"Give me mixed logs (firewall, workstation, server, and cloud authentication logs). Add indicators like impossible travel, brute force, replay attack, suspicious processes. Ask me to analyze and respond."*

### 2.5 Mitigation Techniques

**◆ Lab: Harden an Enterprise Network**

**Prompt:**

*"Provide me a network diagram. Let me apply segmentation, least privilege, patching, allowlisting, and configuration enforcement. Then simulate an attack to see if my mitigations work."*

# DOMAIN 3 — Security Architecture (Labs)

### 3.1 Architecture Models

**◆ Lab: Build a Secure Cloud Architecture**

**Prompt:**

*"Show me a hybrid cloud environment with misconfigurations. Ask me to apply least privilege, secure APIs, proper VPC/VNet segmentation, and correct identity roles."*

### 3.2 Enterprise Infrastructure

**◆ Lab: DMZ & Firewall Configuration**

**Prompt:**

*"Simulate a company building a DMZ with a WAF, IDS/IPS, proxy, VPN, and jump server. Let me design traffic flow rules and test them with sample traffic logs."*

### 3.3 Data Protection

**◆ Lab: Classify and Secure Data**

**Prompt:**

*"Give me sample files, emails, and database entries. Ask me to classify them (public, sensitive, confidential) and choose the correct protections like tokenization, masking, or encryption."*

### 3.4 Resilience & Recovery

**◆ Lab: Disaster Recovery Scenario**

**Prompt:**

*"Simulate a ransomware attack on a hospital. Ask me to choose recovery strategies: snapshots, replication, hot/warm/cold sites. Let me calculate RTO/RPO."*

# DOMAIN 4 — Security Operations (Labs)

**4.1 Baselines & Hardening**

**◆ Lab: Harden a Device**

**Prompt:**

*"Pick a device (server, router, IoT, mobile). Give me a list of vulnerabilities. Ask me to harden it using baselines, patches, firewalls, and least privilege."*

**4.2 Asset Management**

**◆ Lab: Rogue Asset Discovery**

**Prompt:**

*"Simulate a network where unauthorized devices appear. Ask me to find them, classify them, block them, and write a policy for asset control."*

**4.3 Vulnerability Management**

**◆ Lab: Prioritize Vulnerabilities**

**Prompt:**

*"Give me a vulnerability scan with CVSS scores. Ask me to prioritize remediation and justify my decisions."*

**4.4 Monitoring**

**◆ Lab: SIEM Log Investigation**

**Prompt:**

*"Act as a SIEM and provide suspicious events. Ask me to tune alerts, quarantine endpoints, and write a short incident ticket."*

**4.5 Firewall/Email/DNS Security**

**◆ Lab: Firewall Rule Testing**

**Prompt:**

*"Show me firewall rules and traffic logs. Ask me which rules are incorrect and how to fix them to block malicious behavior."*

**4.6 IAM**

◆ **Lab: Create an IAM Policy**

**Prompt:**

*"Simulate AWS/Azure/GCP RBAC roles. Ask me to grant just enough access based on job roles without violating least privilege."*

**4.7 Automation**

◆ **Lab: Build a SOAR Workflow**

**Prompt:**

*"Help me design an automated workflow for phishing detection: SOC receives email → sandbox → SIEM → ticket → quarantine. Ask me to optimize it."*

**4.8 Incident Response**

◆ **Lab: End-to-End Incident Response**

**Prompt:**

*"Simulate an entire IR scenario from detection through recovery. Ask me to fill out each step of the IR plan and perform root cause analysis."*

**4.9 Investigations**

◆ **Lab: Multi-Source Log Correlation**

**Prompt:**

*"Provide logs from firewalls, Linux servers, Windows AD, VPN, cloud services. Ask me to correlate user activity and determine if an insider attack occurred."*

# DOMAIN 5 — Program Management & Oversight (Labs)

**5.1 Governance**

**◆ Lab: Write 3 Security Policies**

**Prompt:**

*"Write an AUP, password policy, and incident response policy."*

**5.2 Risk Management**

**◆ Lab: Calculate Risk (ALE, SLE, ARO)**

**Prompt:**

*"Give me 5 risks with dollar values. Ask me to compute SLE, ARO, ALE, and propose mitigation strategies."*

**5.3 Third-Party Risk**

**◆ Lab: Vendor Risk Assessment**

**Prompt:**

*"Simulate hiring a vendor with questionable security. Ask me to evaluate their SLA, auditability, and supply chain controls."*

**5.4 Compliance**

**◆ Lab: Compliance Review**

**Prompt:**

*"Give me a company operating globally. Ask me to map their data handling to GDPR, HIPAA, and PCI-DSS requirements. Identify violations."*

**5.5 Audits & Assessments**

**◆ Lab: Penetration Test Rules of Engagement**

**Prompt:**

*"Design ROE for a pentest: scope, time windows, targets, tools, reporting, and legal considerations."*

## 5.6 Security Awareness

◆ **Lab: Phishing Simulation**

**Prompt:**

*"Give me five sample emails (some legit, some phishing). Ask me to classify them and explain the red flags."*

# 100-Lab Mega Pack CompTIA Security+ SY0-701 — AI Hands-On Labs

Each lab below is a *copy-ready student prompt*.

---

## DOMAIN 1 — General Security Concepts (Labs 1–10)

---

**Lab 1 — CIA Triad Attack Simulation**

*"Simulate attacks targeting confidentiality, integrity, and availability. Provide logs and ask me to identify which CIA element is affected."*

**Lab 2 — Zero Trust Access Decision Engine**

*"Act as a Zero Trust Policy Engine. Ask me questions about user identity, device health, and risk before deciding allow/deny."*

**Lab 3 — PKI Certificate Lifecycle Hands-On**

*"Walk me through generating a CSR, issuing a certificate, validating OCSP/CRL, and troubleshooting a TLS handshake failure."*

**Lab 4 — Physical Security Penetration Scenario**

*"Create a building with cameras, fencing, bollards, guards, vestibules, and sensors. Challenge me as I try to reach the data center."*

**Lab 5 — Deploying a Honeypot Network**

*"Simulate deploying a honeypot, honeynet, honeyfile, and honeytoken. Show me attacker interactions in a timeline."*

**Lab 6 — Authorization Models in Action**

*"Simulate RBAC, ABAC, MAC, and DAC systems. Ask me to assign permissions and detect flawed policies."*

**Lab 7 — Authentication Systems Lab**

*"Let me authenticate a user using passwords, MFA, certificates, and biometrics. Show failures and let me fix them."*

**Lab 8 — Hashing, Salting, Stretching Workshop**

*"Give me plaintext and let me hash it, salt it, and stretch it. Demonstrate which methods resist attacks."*

**Lab 9 — Gap Analysis Assessment**

*"Provide a fictional company's current security posture. Ask me to perform a gap analysis against best practices."*

**Lab 10 — Cryptographic Failure Simulation**

*"Simulate weak SSL/TLS configs, deprecated ciphers, expired certificates, and let me fix each one."*

# DOMAIN 2 — Threats, Vulnerabilities, and Mitigations (Labs 11–20)

**Lab 11 — Threat Actor Detective**

*"Give me four incidents with clues. Ask me to identify the threat actor and motivation."*

**Lab 12 — Social Engineering Playground**

*"Simulate phishing, vishing, smishing, BEC, and pretexting messages. Ask me to classify each."*

**Lab 13 — Attack Vector Hunt**

*"Create a network with email, USB devices, IoT, misconfigs, cloud apps. Ask me to find all attack vectors."*

**Lab 14 — Vulnerability Identification Lab**

*"Give me sample code, configs, endpoints, and ask me to find vulnerabilities including SQLi, buffer overflow, zero-day."*

**Lab 15 — Live Malware Log Analysis**

*"Provide logs for ransomware, spyware, rootkits, and worms. Ask me to identify the malware family."*

**Lab 16 — Indicators of Compromise (IoC) Investigation**

*"Give me logs with impossible travel, concurrent logins, privilege escalation, and ask me to determine the attack."*

**Lab 17 — Network Attack Reconstruction**

*"Simulate DDoS, on-path attacks, spoofing, DNS poisoning, and ask me to choose mitigations."*

**Lab 18 — Zero-Day Exploitation Scenario**

*"Present a fictional zero-day and ask me to design a response plan before the patch is available."*

**Lab 19 — Misconfiguration Challenge**

*"Give me misconfigured firewalls, IAM roles, API keys, and ask me to fix them."*

**Lab 20 — Hardening the Enterprise**

*"Simulate weak systems and ask me to apply patching, segmentation, allowlisting, and encryption."*

## DOMAIN 3 — Security Architecture (Labs 21–30)

**Lab 21 — Build a DMZ**

*"Help me design a DMZ with WAF, proxy, IPS, and VPN. Ask me to configure inbound/outbound rules."*

**Lab 22 — Secure Cloud Architecture**

*"Give me a compromised hybrid cloud. Ask me to secure IAM roles, networks, VMs, and storage."*

**Lab 23 — Container & Microservices Security**

*"Simulate a microservices environment and let me secure secrets, APIs, and runtime workloads."*

**Lab 24 — Secure IoT Deployment**

*"Provide an IoT network with weak defaults. Ask me to harden onboarding, firmware, keys, and network segmentation."*

**Lab 25 — SCADA/ICS Security Walkthrough**

*"Simulate protecting SCADA from attacks. Let me apply isolation, monitoring, and redundancy."*

**Lab 26 — High Availability & Load Balancing**

*"Let me configure redundancy and failover under multiple outage scenarios."*

**Lab 27 — Data Classification Drill**

*"Give me mixed company data. Ask me to classify and choose proper protections."*

**Lab 28 — Data at Rest vs. Transit vs. In Use**

*"Provide example datasets and ask me how to protect each state of data."*

**Lab 29 — Backup & Recovery Strategy**

*"Ask me to design hot/warm/cold sites, RTO/RPO values, and backup frequencies."*

**Lab 30 — Network Segmentation Challenge**

*"Provide a flat network. Ask me to redesign using VLANs, firewalls, ACLs, and least privilege."*

## DOMAIN 4 — Security Operations (Labs 31–45)

**Lab 31 — Secure Baseline Creation**

*"Let me build secure baselines for Windows, Linux, and cloud VMs."*

**Lab 32 — Hardening a Router/Switch**

*"Simulate a switch with open ports, default credentials, and ask me to harden it."*

**Lab 33 — Harden Mobile Devices**

*"Provide mobile security scenarios involving MDM, BYOD, COPE, Bluetooth risks, and app controls."*

**Lab 34 — Incident Response Lifecycle**

*"Simulate an entire IR scenario from preparation to lessons learned."*

**Lab 35 — SIEM Triage Lab**

*"Show me SIEM alerts and ask me to categorize severity and response."*

**Lab 36 — Firewall Rule Optimization**

*"Give me a messy firewall rule set and ask me to optimize rules and block attacks."*

**Lab 37 — Email Security Lab**

*"Simulate DKIM, SPF, DMARC failures and ask me to fix mail spoofing issues."*

**Lab 38 — DNS Security Investigation**

*"Provide DNS logs showing exfiltration, tunneling, or poisoning and ask me to detect them."*

**Lab 39 — Identity and Access Misuse**

*"Simulate IAM roles that violate least privilege. Ask me to fix over-permissive identities."*

**Lab 40 — PAM & JIT Access**

*"Allow me to assign temporary elevated privileges to staff and audit misuse."*

**Lab 41 — Password Security Analysis**

*"Give me passwords to analyze for length, salt, reuse, complexity."*

**Lab 42 — Network Access Control Simulation**

*"Simulate NAC onboarding. Ask me to classify devices as compliant or non-compliant."*

**Lab 43 — Endpoint Detection Response (EDR)**

*"Provide EDR detections, quarantines, and let me investigate suspicious processes."*

**Lab 44 — Vulnerability Scan Interpretation**

*"Give me scan results and ask me to differentiate false positives, CVSS scores, priorities."*

**Lab 45 — Log Correlation Across Systems**

*"Provide logs from VPN, AD, Linux, firewall, cloud. Ask me to correlate events."*

## DOMAIN 5 — Program Management & Oversight (Labs 46–50)

**Lab 46 — Policy Writing Workshop**

*"Ask me to write an Acceptable Use Policy, Password Policy, and Incident Response Policy."*

**Lab 47 — Risk Management Calculations**

*"Give me risks with dollar impacts. Ask me to calculate SLE, ARO, ALE."*

**Lab 48 — Vendor Risk Assessment**

*"Simulate onboarding a vendor. Ask me to evaluate SLA, audit logs, supply chain dependencies."*

**Lab 49 — Compliance Mapping Challenge**

*"Ask me to map company data flows to GDPR/HIPAA/PCI requirements and find violations."*

**Lab 50 — Internal Audit Simulation**

*"Perform an internal audit. Give me findings to categorize as high/medium/low risk with recommendations."*

# CompTIA Security+ SY0-701 — 100-Lab Expansion Pack (Labs 51–100)

These are brand-new labs not included in the first 50.

---

## DOMAIN 1 — General Security Concepts (Labs 51–60)

---

**Lab 51 — Deep Dive into Control Types**

*"Give me six security controls (preventive, detective, corrective, compensating, directive, deterrent). Ask me to classify 12 examples into the correct category with justification."*

**Lab 52 — Zero Trust Microsegmentation Lab**

*"Design a microsegments inside a Zero Trust network. Prompt me to isolate users, apps, and data while testing potential attack paths."*

**Lab 53 — Authentication Attack Simulation**

*"Simulate password spraying, brute force, credential stuffing, and MFA fatigue. Ask me to detect and stop each attack."*

**Lab 54 — Physical Sensor Calibration**

*"Give me a virtual room with multiple sensors (infrared, microwave, ultrasonic, pressure). Ask me to place each sensor in the proper location based on threats."*

**Lab 55 — Public Key vs. Private Key Challenge**

*"Give me multiple use-case scenarios and ask me to determine whether to use symmetric, asymmetric, hashing, or hybrid encryption."*

**Lab 56 — Build-a-Policy: Access Control Policy**

*"Create an access control policy including password rules, MFA, authorization model, and logging."*

**Lab 57 — Hash Collision Exploration**

*"Simulate weak hashing algorithms. Let me experiment with collisions and strengthen the environment."*

**Lab 58 — Data Masking Lab**

*"Provide sample customer data. Ask me to perform masking, tokenization, and partial obfuscation based on compliance rules."*

**Lab 59 — Honey Network Strategy Exercise**

*"Give me different network types and ask me where and why to deploy honeypots and honeytokens."*

**Lab 60 — Building a Zero Trust Identity Engine**

*"Create risk-based access policies with adaptive identity and contextual analysis."*

## DOMAIN 2 — Threats, Vulnerabilities, and Mitigations (Labs 61–75)

**Lab 61 — Email Threat Dissection**

*"Provide multiple emails with hidden indicators (links, headers, spoofing). Ask me to dissect and classify threats."*

**Lab 62 — Supply Chain Risk Simulation**

*"Simulate a vendor compromise (like SolarWinds). Ask me to detect, isolate, and respond."*

**Lab 63 — Mobile Malware Detection**

*"Provide mobile device behaviors and ask me to identify spyware, jailbreaking, sideloading, and indicators of compromise."*

**Lab 64 — DDoS Defense Strategy**

*"Simulate a DDoS attack. Ask me to implement rules on firewalls, load balancers, and CDNs."*

**Lab 65 — Cloud Misconfiguration Hunt**

*"Give me a cloud environment with weak IAM roles, open buckets, and exposed APIs. Ask me to secure it."*

**Lab 66 — Exploiting & Patching a Vulnerable Web App**

*"Simulate SQLi, XSS, and directory traversal. Ask me to patch each vulnerability."*

**Lab 67 — Insider Threat Detection**

*"Provide logs and behavior analysis. Let me identify insider threats from normal employees."*

**Lab 68 — Rogue Device Identification**

*"Simulate rogue APs, unauthorized IoT devices, and BYOD violations. Ask me to find and isolate them."*

**Lab 69 — Malware Reverse Engineering (Conceptual)**

*"Give me a malware behavior description and ask me to determine indicators of compromise."*

**Lab 70 — Credential Harvesting Scenario**

*"Provide a fake login page and logs. Ask me to detect credential harvesting attempts."*

**Lab 71 — Advanced Phishing Campaign**

*"Simulate spear-phishing, clone phishing, and whaling. Ask me to classify each attempt."*

**Lab 72 — Zero-Day Response Drill**

*"Give me a situation where a zero-day affects a critical system. Ask me to build a response plan."*

**Lab 73 — Human Vulnerability Mapping**

*"Analyze social engineering susceptibility and create training recommendations."*

**Lab 74 — Patch Management Challenge**

*"Simulate out-of-date systems. Ask me to prioritize patches based on severity and business impact."*

**Lab 75 — Browser Exploit Forensics**

*"Present suspicious browser events and ask me to identify malicious extensions and scripts."*

## DOMAIN 3 — Security Architecture (Labs 76–85)

**Lab 76 — Create a Secure Network Topology**

*"Give me a blank network diagram and ask me to design a secure topology with zones, DMZ, and segmentation."*

**Lab 77 — Configure a WAF (Web Application Firewall)**

*"Give me a list of web traffic patterns. Ask me to create WAF rules that block malicious activity."*

**Lab 78 — Secure API Gateway Setup**

*"Simulate insecure APIs. Ask me to apply authentication, rate limiting, and logging."*

**Lab 79 — SDN Security Controls**

*"Let me configure SDN policies and segment flows while defending against an on-path attacker."*

**Lab 80 — Identity Federation Lab**

*"Simulate SAML, OAuth, and OIDC. Ask me to configure SSO for a fictional company."*

**Lab 81 — Data Loss Prevention Strategy**

*"Ask me to design a DLP solution for email, cloud storage, and endpoints."*

**Lab 82 — Secure Virtualization Deployment**

*"Give me hosts and VMs. Ask me to prevent VM escape, isolate hypervisors, and enforce snapshots."*

**Lab 83 — IoT Network Vulnerability Walkthrough**

*"Simulate IoT devices with weak defaults. Ask me to secure them."*

**Lab 84 — Build a Multi-Cloud Security Strategy**

*"Simulate AWS + Azure + GCP environments. Ask me to unify IAM, logs, and segmentation."*

**Lab 85 — SCADA Failover Testing**

*"Simulate failures in a SCADA system and ask me to ensure resilience."*

## DOMAIN 4 — Security Operations (Labs 86–100)

**Lab 86 — Deep Log Analysis Marathon**

*"Give me 20 logs from varied systems and ask me to identify all suspicious events."*

**Lab 87 — EDR vs. Antivirus Comparison Drill**

*"Simulate threats and ask me which tool (EDR or AV) detects them and why."*

**Lab 88 — Windows Event Log Investigation**

*"Provide event logs and ask me to trace an attacker's path through a Windows domain."*

**Lab 89 — Linux Log Forensics**

*"Give me auth.log, syslog, and bash history entries. Ask me to detect malicious actions."*

**Lab 90 — Cloud IAM Drift Lab**

*"Simulate IAM drift where permissions increase over time. Ask me to fix it."*

**Lab 91 — SOAR Playbook Creation**

*"Ask me to build a playbook for malware detection and containment using automation."*

**Lab 92 — Incident Documentation Exercise**

*"Simulate an incident and ask me to fill out an IR report."*

**Lab 93 — Secure Protocol Selection Lab**

*"Give me insecure protocols and ask me to replace them with secure alternatives."*

**Lab 94 — Endpoint Hardening Challenge**

*"Provide weak workstation configs and ask me to harden them."*

**Lab 95 — DLP Incident Response**

*"Simulate accidental sensitive data exposure and ask me to respond."*

**Lab 96 — Network Traffic PCAP Lab**

*"Provide a mock PCAP summary and ask me to detect anomalies."*

**Lab 97 — Email Header Analysis**

*"Provide full email headers. Ask me to find spoofing, misroutes, and authentication failures."*

**Lab 98 — Privilege Escalation Detection**

*"Give me logs where a user escalates privileges. Ask me to respond and prevent recurrence."*

**Lab 99 — SIEM Alert Tuning Workshop**

*"Give me noisy alerts and ask me to tune them to reduce false positives."*

**Lab 100 — Final Cyber Range Simulation**

*"Simulate a complete enterprise breach: phishing → lateral movement → exfiltration. Ask me to walk through every defense step."*

# AI Image Generation Prompts for Security+ Visual Learning

## How to Use These Prompts

Copy and paste these prompts into AI image generators like *Google Gemini, Midjourney, DALL-E 3, Stable Diffusion, or Bing Image Creator*. Adjust as needed for your specific tool. I have created for some of the chapters and will leave it to you to create and try your own prompts, cheers.

*Chapter 1: Security Controls*

**Prompt 1:** "Infographic showing the CIA triad: Confidentiality as a locked safe with a keyhole, Integrity as a perfect unbroken chain, and Availability as a 24/7 neon 'OPEN' sign. Clean, modern, corporate style. White background."

**Prompt 2:** "3D diagram of security control types: Preventive (a brick wall), Detective (a security camera with red blinking light), Corrective (a first aid kit), Deterrent ('Beware of Dog' sign), Compensating (a backup generator), Directive (an arrow sign). Each icon floating with labels."

**Prompt 3:** "Matrix/grid comparing technical, managerial, operational, and physical security controls. Technical = firewall icon, Managerial = policy document, Operational = person doing a task, Physical = lock and key. Color-coded, minimalist design."

*Chapter 2: Threat Actors*

**Prompt 4:** "Character lineup of different threat actors: Nation-state as a shadowy figure with a flag on the shoulder, Organized crime as a business suit with a skull tie, Hacktivist wearing a Guy Fawkes mask with a laptop, Insider threat as an employee with two faces (smiling and sinister). Comic book style, dramatic lighting."

**Prompt 5:** "Mind map showing threat actor motivations branching out: Financial gain (dollar signs), Espionage (spyglass), Disruption (broken server), Revenge (angry face), Philosophical beliefs (raised fist). Central node: 'Motivations'. Clean, flowing lines."

*Chapter 4: Cryptography*

**Prompt 6:** "Visual comparison: Symmetric encryption showing a single key locking and unlocking a chest. Asymmetric encryption showing a public key locking the chest and a different private key unlocking it. Side-by-side, clear arrows, technical illustration style."

**Prompt 7:** "Animated concept frame: Digital signature process. 1) Document with hash value below. 2) Private key encrypting the hash. 3) Encrypted hash attached as signature. 4) Public key decrypting to verify. Diagram with numbered steps."

**Prompt 8:** "PKI hierarchy visualization: Root CA at top as a giant anchor, Intermediate CAs as smaller anchors below, end certificates as ships secured by chains. Ocean background, metaphor for trust."

*Chapter 7: Vulnerabilities*

**Prompt 9:** "Buffer overflow explained visually: A glass (buffer) being overfilled with water, the water spilling over into adjacent memory spaces where it overwrites instructions (represented as scrambled code). Technical illustration."

**Prompt 10:** "SQL injection attack diagram: A web form with text field showing: 'Username: admin' 'Password: ' OR '1'='1'. The input flowing into a database, with malicious SQL commands highlighted in red as they bypass authentication."

**Prompt 11:** "Cross-site scripting (XSS) visualization: A malicious script tag <script>steal_cookies()</script> being injected into a comment on a webpage. The script executing in other users' browsers, depicted as cookie icons being stolen. Web interface style."

*Chapter 10: Architecture Models*

**Prompt 12:** "Shared responsibility model for cloud IaaS, PaaS, SaaS: Three columns showing what the customer manages vs. what the cloud provider manages, with a sliding scale. IaaS = customer manages more, SaaS = provider manages more. Clean corporate graphic."

**Prompt 13:** "Container vs Virtual Machine architecture: Left side showing containers (multiple colored boxes) sharing one OS kernel (a single foundation). Right side showing VMs (multiple complete computers) each with their own OS on a hypervisor. Side-by-side comparison."

**Prompt 14:** "Zero Trust architecture diagram: No perimeter. Multiple micro-segments (small castles), each requiring verification at the gate. User trying to access resources, being verified at multiple checkpoints. 'Never trust, always verify' as central motto."

*Chapter 11: Network Security*

**Prompt 15:** "Network segmentation visualization: Flat network (one big room where fire spreads everywhere) vs. Segmented network (multiple rooms with firewalls as fire doors containing the blaze). Fire metaphor, easy to understand."

**Prompt 16:** "Firewall types comparison: Packet-filtering firewall (inspecting envelopes only), Stateful firewall (tracking conversations), NGFW (deep inspection looking inside envelopes). Post office metaphor, progressive detail."

**Prompt 17:** "DMZ (Demilitarized Zone) network diagram: Internet cloud → Firewall → DMZ zone with web/mail servers → Internal firewall → Internal network with workstations and databases. Clear zoning with different trust levels."

*Chapter 13: Resilience & Recovery*

**Prompt 18:** "Business continuity site types: Hot site (identical building with same people working), Warm site (building ready but empty desks), Cold site (empty warehouse). Three-panel comic showing recovery speed vs. cost."

**Prompt 19:** "RTO vs RPO visualization: Timeline showing a disaster point. RPO = how much data loss back in time (hourglass). RTO = how long to restore (clock). Simple, powerful icons with clear definitions."

**Prompt 20:** "3-2-1 Backup Rule infographic: 3 total copies of data, on 2 different media types (hard drive + tape + cloud), with 1 copy offsite. Visual counting graphic with icons."

*Chapter 16: Vulnerability Management*

**Prompt 21:** "CVSS scoring meter/gauge: 0.0-3.9 = Low (green), 4.0-6.9 = Medium (yellow), 7.0-8.9 = High (orange), 9.0-10.0 = Critical (red). Needle pointing to Critical zone with examples of CVSS 9.8 vulnerabilities."

**Prompt 22:** "Vulnerability management lifecycle: Continuous circle with arrows: Identify → Assess → Prioritize → Remediate → Verify → Report. Each step with representative icon. Circular flowchart."

*Chapter 19: Identity & Access Management*

**Prompt 23:** "MFA factors visualization: Something you KNOW (brain icon with password), Something you HAVE (smartphone with authenticator app), Something you ARE (fingerprint scan), Somewhere you ARE (location pin). Four quadrants."

**Prompt 24:** "SSO/SAML flow diagram: User → Service Provider (SP) → Redirect to Identity Provider (IdP) → Authentication → SAML Assertion back to SP → Access granted. Sequence diagram with arrows."

**Prompt 25:** "Role-Based Access Control (RBAC) hierarchy: Organization chart showing CEO → Departments → Roles → Users. Permissions attached to roles, not individuals. Clean organizational diagram."

*Chapter 21: Incident Response*

**Prompt 26:** "Incident response lifecycle: 7-stage circular diagram: Preparation (toolkit), Detection (alarm bell), Analysis (magnifying glass), Containment (quarantine sign), Eradication (bug spray), Recovery (reboot icon), Lessons Learned (notebook). Continuous improvement cycle."

**Prompt 27:** "Forensic chain of custody visualization: Evidence bag with tag showing sequential signatures: Collector → Analyst → Storage → Court. Each transfer documented. Legal/forensic style."

*Chapter 24: Risk Management*

**Prompt 28:** "Risk calculation formulas illustrated: SLE = Asset Value × Exposure Factor, ARO = annual frequency, ALE = SLE × ARO. Mathematical equations with visual examples: Server worth $10,000 with 25% exposure factor = $2,500 SLE."

**Prompt 29:** "Risk treatment strategies: Avoid (roadblock icon), Mitigate (shield), Transfer (insurance document), Accept (checkmark). Four options with simple metaphors."

Chapter 28: Security Awareness

**Prompt 30:** "Phishing email red flags visual checklist: 1) Suspicious sender (question mark), 2) Urgent language (alarm clock), 3) Generic greeting ('Dear Customer'), 4) Mismatched links (hover effect shown), 5) Request for credentials (keyhole). Checklist format."

**Prompt 31:** "Human firewall concept: Employees as literal bricks in a firewall wall, each with a security awareness shield. Breaches happening where bricks are missing or weak. Powerful metaphor visualization."

**Prompt 32:** "Defense in Depth visualization: Like an onion with multiple layers: Perimeter security → Network security → Host security → Application security → Data security. Each layer providing protection."

**Prompt 33:** "Password strength visualization: Weak password = short, simple key easily picked. Strong passphrase = long, complex key that's virtually unpickable. Lock and key metaphor."

**Prompt 34:** "Social engineering techniques: Phishing (fishing rod with email hook), Pretexting (actor with mask), Baiting (USB stick as bait), Tailgating (person slipping through door). Four-panel cartoon."

**Prompt 35:** "Encryption at rest vs. in transit: Data at rest = encrypted hard drive with lock icon. Data in transit = encrypted tunnel (VPN) with data packets flowing through secured pipe."

**Tips for Better Results:**

1. **Add style descriptors:** "corporate infographic," "technical diagram," "clean minimalist design," "3D illustration," "comic book style"
2. **Specify aspect ratio:** "16:9 for presentation," "1:1 for social media," "4:3 for documents"
3. **Use negative prompts:** "no text," "no watermark," "no blurry"
4. **Iterate:** Generate, then refine: "same concept but more detailed," "more professional"
5. **Combine concepts:** "Create a mind map showing all attack vectors from chapter 6"

**Remember:** These AI tools are constantly improving. If a prompt doesn't work perfectly, try rephrasing or simplifying. The goal is to create visual aids that make abstract security concepts concrete and memorable for your study process.

# Appendix B: Essential Glossary

Building Your Security Vocabulary

💡 **AI STUDY TIP:** This glossary contains the most frequent terms on the exam. However, if you encounter a word that isn't listed here, use this prompt to generate a custom definition:

*"Define the term [Insert Word]. Explain it in the context of cybersecurity and give me one real-world example of how it is used."*

A

- **AAA (Authentication, Authorization, Accounting):** The framework for controlling access. (Who are you? What can you do? What did you do?).
- **ACL (Access Control List):** A list of rules (usually on a firewall or router) that permits or denies traffic based on IP addresses or ports.
- **Advanced Persistent Threat (APT):** A sophisticated, long-term attacker (usually a Nation-State) that maintains access to a network to steal data over time.
- **Air Gap:** A physical security control where a device is physically disconnected from all other networks (including the internet) to prevent hacking.
- **ALE (Annualized Loss Expectancy):** The expected monetary loss for an asset over one year due to a specific risk. Formula: SLE x ARO.

B

- **Blue Team:** The defensive security team responsible for protecting the organization, patching vulnerabilities, and monitoring logs.
- **Botnet:** A network of infected computers ("zombies") controlled by a hacker, often used to launch DDoS attacks.
- **Brute Force Attack:** A trial-and-error method of cracking passwords by guessing every possible combination.

C

- **CIA Triad:** The three main goals of security: **Confidentiality** (Secrecy), **Integrity** (Accuracy), and **Availability** (Uptime).
- **Cold Site:** A disaster recovery facility that has power and space but no hardware or data. It takes the longest to bring online.

- **CVE (Common Vulnerabilities and Exposures):** A standardized list of known security flaws in software, each assigned a unique ID number (e.g., CVE-2025-1234).

**D**

- **DDoS (Distributed Denial of Service):** An attack that floods a server with traffic from many different sources to crash it and deny access to legitimate users.
- **DLP (Data Loss Prevention):** Software that detects and blocks sensitive data (like Credit Card numbers) from leaving the corporate network.
- **DMZ (Demilitarized Zone):** A semi-trusted network zone between the internet and the internal network. Public-facing servers (Web, Email) are placed here.

**E**

- **Encryption:** The process of converting readable data (plaintext) into unreadable characters (ciphertext) using a mathematical key.
- **Exploit:** Code or a technique that takes advantage of a vulnerability to breach a system.

**F**

- **False Positive:** When a security tool (like an IDS) triggers an alert for benign (safe) activity.
- **Firewall:** A network security device that monitors and filters traffic based on established security rules.

**G**

- **Gap Analysis:** A comparison between the current state of security and the desired state (or regulatory requirement).

**H**

- **Hashing:** A one-way mathematical function that converts data into a fixed-length string. Used to verify **Integrity**.
- **Honeypot:** A decoy system designed to lure attackers away from critical systems and study their behavior.
- **Hot Site:** A fully operational disaster recovery site with real-time data replication. It allows for near-instant recovery.

**I**

- **IaaS (Infrastructure as a Service):** Cloud model where the vendor provides the hardware (storage, servers), but the customer manages the Operating System and Software (e.g., AWS EC2).
- **Incident Response (IR):** The organized approach to addressing and managing the aftermath of a security breach (Preparation, Identification, Containment, Eradication, Recovery, Lessons Learned).
- **Insider Threat:** A security risk that originates from within the organization (e.g., employees, contractors).

**L**

- **Least Privilege:** The principle that users should be granted the minimum level of access necessary to perform their job functions.

**M**

- **Malware:** Malicious software designed to cause damage. Includes Viruses, Worms, Trojans, and Ransomware.
- **MFA (Multi-Factor Authentication):** An authentication method that requires two or more verification factors (Something you know, have, or are).
- **Man-in-the-Middle (MitM):** An attack where the attacker secretly intercepts and relays communications between two parties.

**N**

- **Non-Repudiation:** The assurance that the sender of information is provided with proof of delivery and the recipient is provided with proof of the sender's identity (sender cannot deny sending).

**P**

- **Penetration Testing (Pen Test):** An authorized simulated cyberattack on a computer system, performed to evaluate the security of the system.
- **Phishing:** A social engineering attack that uses fraudulent emails to trick users into revealing sensitive information.
- **PKI (Public Key Infrastructure):** The framework of encryption, digital certificates, and Certificate Authorities (CAs) that secures communication on the internet.

**R**

- **Ransomware:** Malware that encrypts a victim's files and demands payment for the decryption key.
- **Red Team:** Ethical hackers who simulate attacks to test the effectiveness of the Blue Team's defenses.
- **Risk:** The potential for loss, damage, or destruction of an asset as a result of a threat exploiting a vulnerability.
- **Rootkit:** Malicious software designed to hide the existence of other malware and maintain privileged (root) access to a system.

**S**

- **Salting:** Adding random data to a password before hashing it to protect against Rainbow Table attacks.
- **SIEM (Security Information and Event Management):** A solution that collects and analyzes log data from across the network to detect threats.
- **Social Engineering:** The psychological manipulation of people into performing actions or divulging confidential information.
- **SQL Injection (SQLi):** An injection attack that makes it possible to execute malicious SQL statements that control a database server.

**T**

- **Trojan Horse:** A type of malware that disguises itself as legitimate software.
- **Zero Day:** A vulnerability that is unknown to the software vendor or has no patch available yet.
- **Zero Trust:** A security model that assumes no user or device is trustworthy, regardless of their location (inside or outside the network).

**To the Future Defenders of the Digital World**

If you are reading this, you have likely reached the end of our journey together. You have navigated the complexities of cryptography, dissected network architectures, and learned to think like both a hacker and a defender.

But before you close this book and schedule your exam, I want to leave you with one final thought.

**The certification is just the beginning.**

Passing the CompTIA Security+ exam proves you have the knowledge. But in the real world, knowledge alone is not enough. The threat landscape changes every single day. The "secure" protocols of today will be the vulnerabilities of tomorrow. The tools we use now will be obsolete in five years.

This is why I wrote this book with a focus on *Artificial Intelligence.*

My goal was not just to help you memorize port numbers or acronyms. My goal was to teach you how to be *adaptable*. By learning how to leverage AI as a tool, you have future-proofed your career. You now have the ability to learn faster, simulate scenarios instantly, and solve problems that don't even exist yet.

However, never forget the human element. AI can spot a pattern, but it takes a human to understand *context*. AI can write code, but it takes a human to understand *ethics*.

You are entering a field that requires integrity, curiosity, and resilience. You are the guardians of our data, our privacy, and our infrastructure. It is a heavy responsibility, but I know you are ready for it.

Go take that exam. Crush it. And then, keep learning.

See you in the field.

**Professor Ifti** *Seek Knowledge | Enhance Skills*

Thank you for purchasing this amazing book. Please email me your order information, and I will send you the PDF version of **Part II**, which will allow you to easily copy and paste the prompts for your use.

You can reach me at *Learn@Professorifti.com*

With best regards,

**Professor Ifti**

www.ingramcontent.com/pod-product-compliance
Lightning Source LLC
LaVergne TN
LVHW071343210926
848486LV00003B/220
* 9 7 9 8 2 9 5 6 3 3 2 3 2 *